SMARTER CHARTS
for Math, Science & Social Studies

Making Learning Visible in the Content Areas

K–2

ANATOMY OF A CHART

What makes a smarter chart? Lots of things! Like a recipe that needs a pinch of sugar and a handful of flour, charts are composed of a few components that work together in harmony. Instructional charts may not be rocket science, but they use brain science to create high-impact aids for young mathematicians, scientists, and social scientists.

Materials

Like any artist, a chart maker benefits from tools of the trade: chart paper and markers. But there is more—a restickable glue stick and colored copy paper can change charts from wall hangings to living things. Color-coding using colored paper, sticky notes, and markers helps make each strategy clear and distinct, which aids memory.

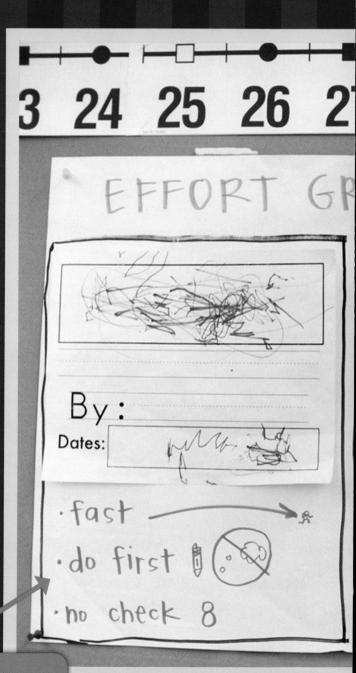

Language

The language on your chart reflects the reading level and language competency of the students you teach. Make it like a billboard; don't write a lot when a little gets the point across. The words on the chart should be easily read and understood by the majority of your students.

Content

Charts take abstract content and represent it in a concrete way to support independence. This chart about effort provides tips for being more thoughtful and aware as children work. It reflects instruction by stating explicit strategies, showing the process of how to do something, or giving examples.

Chart Heading

Headings are the advertisement for your chart. Written large and legibly, they invite thinkers in, name a big skill, and set your students up to utilize the rest of the chart. They grab attention with a strong statement or a question.

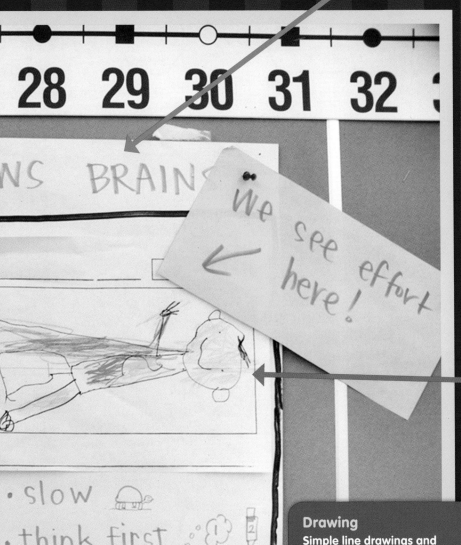

WS BRAIN

We see effort ← here!

• slow
• think first
• check

Broken Pencils!

Broken pencils

Student Art

The best teachers are often in your classroom—the students and the work they create! There is nothing more engaging to students than seeing their work celebrated and elevated as a mentor for others. Placing student exemplars and examples reinforces expectations and provides models that are within the zone of proximal development of the other students in the classroom.

Drawing

Simple line drawings and sketches communicate vast amounts of information to young children. When used in tandem with a few wisely chosen words, pictures support high-level thinking, define new concepts and words, and provide additional information. Drawings make the chart engaging and enhance meaning. Photographs and clip art can also be used effectively.

1. How big is this problem?

Glitch | Bummer | Disaster!

Math Charts

Hexagon

6 sides

6 corners

Double-Digit Addition.

$$31 + 14 = ?$$

Build then check   10,20, 30,31 ✓

Build then check   10,11, 12,13, 14 ✓

How many all together?

$$31 + 14 = 45$$

Subtraction Actions!

Draw a picture

13   -9

Use objects (manipulatives)

Count back

13, 12, 11, 10, 9, 8, 7, 6, 5, (4)

Use a number line

1 2 3 4 5 6 7 8 9 10 11 12 13 14

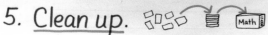

We are serious about math games.

1. <u>Decide</u> what to play.   cards cubes beads
2. <u>Read</u> the rules.   1. First... 2. Then 3. Next 4. Last.
3. <u>Set up</u> the game.
4. <u>PLAY</u>, PLAY, PLAY!
5. <u>Clean up.</u>   Math

Science Charts

Exemplar Chart

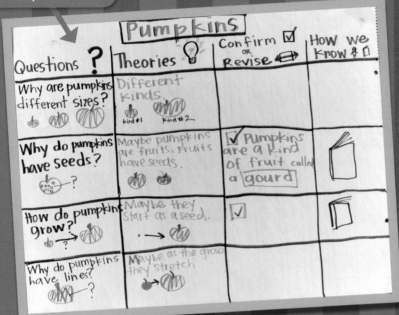

Pumpkins

Questions ?	Theories 💡	Confirm ☑ or Revise	How we Know 📖
Why are pumpkins different sizes?	Different kinds. kind #1 kind #2		
Why do pumpkins have seeds?	Maybe pumpkins are fruits. Fruits have seeds.	☑ Pumpkins are a kind of fruit called a gourd	
How do pumpkins grow?	Maybe they start as a seed.	☑	
Why do pumpkins have lines?	Maybe as the grow they stretch		

Concept Chart

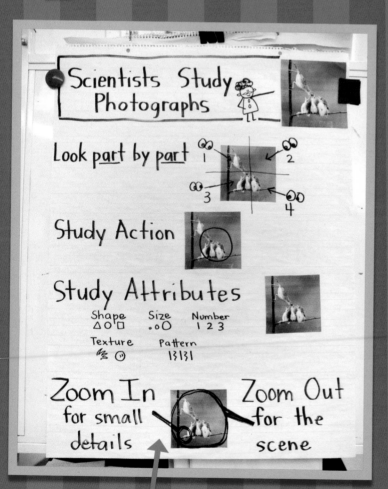

Scientists Study Photographs

Look part by part   1 2 3 4

Study Action

Study Attributes

Shape △ ○ □   Size ∘∘○   Number 1 2 3

Texture   Pattern 13131

Zoom In for small details   **Zoom Out** for the scene

Repertoire Chart

Ready, Set ... EXPERIMENT!

1. Read: Materials

   Cotton Ball   Straw   Wood Block   Tape

2. Decide: I will get _____
   * Be careful!!

3. Reread Materials

   Cotton Ball   Straw   Wood Block   Tape

4. Check: Did we get it all?

   ✓ ✓ Wood Block ✓

Routine Chart

Social Studies Charts

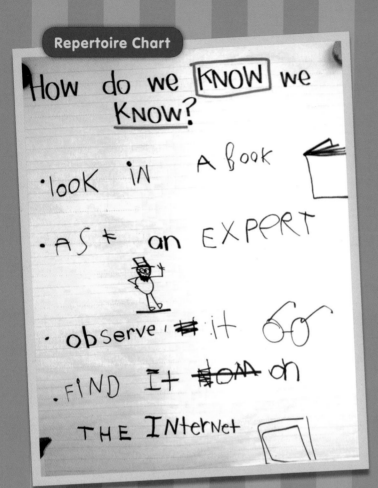

How do we KNOW we KNOW?

- look in A Book
- AS† an EXPERT
- observe it
- FIND It on THE INTernet

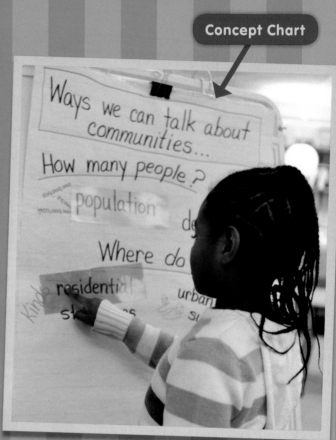

Ways we can talk about communities...

How many people?

population

Where do

residential   urban

Be **STRATEGIC**

1. Think
2. Plan
3. Do

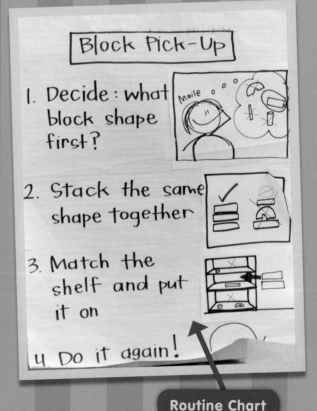

Block Pick-Up

1. Decide: what block shape first?
2. Stack the same shape together
3. Match the shelf and put it on
4. Do it again!

Literacy Charts

Routine Chart

Exemplar Chart

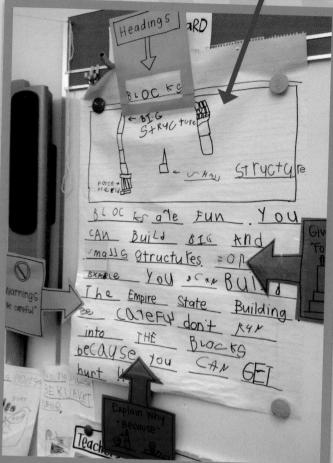

Process Chart

Routine Chart

Social Emotional Learning Charts

Process Chart

Solution Center

1. How big is this problem?

| Glitch | Bummer | Disaster! |

2. Say how you feel

I feel

because...

sad | mad | stop! annoyed | frustrated

Process Chart

How To Give a Compliment

Say Someone's Name.   Evan

Look in their eyes.

Say something Nice.

Repertoire Chart

Concept Chart

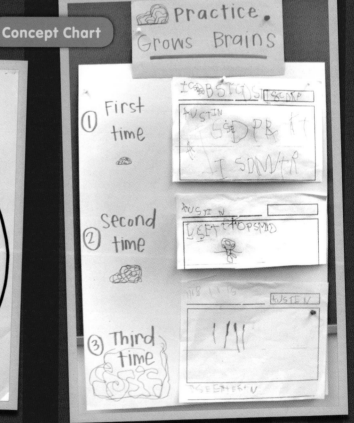

Use your words

Use iMessage

I feel _____ when you _____

Apologize   I'm sorry

Tell them to stop   STOP

Practice Grows Brains

① First time

② Second time

③ Third time

SMARTER CHARTS

for Math, Science & Social Studies

Making Learning Visible in the Content Areas   K-2

Kristine Mraz * Marjorie Martinelli

HEINEMANN
Portsmouth, NH

Heinemann

361 Hanover Street

Portsmouth, NH 03801–3912

www.heinemann.com

Offices and agents throughout the world

The authors and publisher wish to thank those who have generously given permission to reprint borrowed material:

Excerpts from Common Core State Standards © Copyright 2010. National Governors Association Center for Best Practices and Council of Chief State School Officers. All rights reserved.

Library of Congress Cataloging-in-Publication Data

Mraz, Kristine.

    Smarter charts for math, science, and social studies : making learning visible in the content areas / Kristine Mraz & Marjorie Martinelli.

        pages cm.

    Includes bibliographical references.

    ISBN 978-0-325-05662-3

    1. Visual education. 2. Content area reading—Study and teaching (Elementary)—Audio-visual aids. 3. Mathematics—Study and teaching (Elementary)—Audio-visual aids. 4. Science—Study and teaching (Elementary)—Audio-visual aids. 5. Social sciences—Study and teaching (Elementary)—Audio-visual aids. 6. Charts, diagrams, etc. I. Martinelli, Marjorie. II. Title.

    LB1043.5.M345 2014

    371.33'5—dc23

                            2014011075

Editor: Zoë Ryder White

Production: Patty Adams

Cover and interior design: Monica Ann Crigler

Cover and interior photographer: Jesse Angelo

Typesetter: Gina Poirier Design

Manufacturing: Steve Bernier

Printed in the United States of America on acid-free paper

18 17 16 15 14 EBM 1 2 3 4 5

Contents

Acknowledgments

First of all, this book would not have happened if it were not for the thousands of teachers around the world who sent us their encouragement and questions via emails, tweets, blogs, and Facebook. It would not have happened without those teachers we work with directly, who have allowed us to ask questions and to try out ideas in their classrooms. Without all of you, we would be two ladies with a lot of markers and not much else. Seeing how children interact with the charts has also been a source of inspiration and delight. Thank you for inspiring us with all that you do in the classroom and in the world.

Huge thanks and gratitude go to the teachers and administration at PS 59 who have volunteered their time, their brains, their passion, their charting talents, and their photogenic faces to this book. Kathryn Cazes and Mollie Gaffney Smith run the most inspired Integrated Co-Teaching (ICT) classroom we have seen to date. Two more passionate special educators we could not hope to find. Katie Lee brings heart and soul to her classroom. One cannot walk into her room without an immediate exhalation of tension and stress and inhalation of the calm and compassionate atmosphere she cultivates. Valerie Geschwind is the kind of teacher who lives in the backseat, trusting her students to drive instruction. Watching her as she watches children is an exercise in inspiration. Adele Schroeter, principal, and Alison Porcelli, assistant principal, are two of the most ethical, fearless, and compassionate leaders we have seen. They steer their ship in whatever direction is best for children and their teachers, regardless of what storms may blow. Thanks also to Sarah Hang, Karly Frigenti, Jennifer Maravi, Judy Londa, and Jeannie Kim for loaning us their classrooms, their charts, and their kindness.

We feel truly blessed to have the same team of brilliant professionals brought back together for *Smarter Charts for Math, Science, and Social Studies.* Zoë Ryder White, our beloved editor of *Smarter Charts*, not only returned as our editor for *Smarter Charts for Math, Science, and Social Studies* but was our biggest cheerleader, promoter, and supporter every step of the way. Zoë is compassion made human. Patty Adams and Monica Crigler designed our layout and cover, turning Times New Roman into something beautiful and powerful. We thank them for their enthusiasm and creativity. We also thank them for understanding the power of a good visual, and a good pen.

Tremendous gratitude goes to Jesse Angelo for agreeing to be our photographer again and for photographing the children, teachers, and charts with such sensitivity and grace. New to our team this year but making us all the smarter is the indomitable Katherine Bryant, math and science guru/editor at Heinemann. Katherine lent us her mind for details big and small, and for her we are grateful.

We have learned much from the work that the Teachers College Reading and Writing Project has been exploring around literacy in social studies and science. Besides being at the forefront of workshop teaching, our colleagues and collaborators have taught us a great deal about the power of community. We thank them all for their support, for their generosity with their knowledge, and for the work they do to promote best practices in the world at large.

Thank you to our families and friends who continued to provide mammoth support each and every day, despite canceled dinner dates and unreturned phones calls.

Marjorie could not do what she does as a staff developer, presenter, and writer if it were not for her husband, Tom, who patiently delays dinner for her, puts on jazz to calm the world, and listens with care and understanding. Her daughters, Katherine and Christina, are a forever source of joy and happiness and are wise beyond their years. Marjorie also appreciates the pride her extended family has in her accomplishments, especially her sister Barbara, kindergarten teacher extraordinaire; her sister Holly, who cares for the world; and her mother, Jeanne, who always manages to turn lemons into lemonade.

Kristi would like to (again) thank her team and administration at PS 59. With them she has found a home that challenges her mind, encourages her eccentricity, and has taught her more about teamwork than any sport she tried to play. Kristi would also like to thank her kindergarten students and their amazing families. Their joy, passion, and dedication is nothing short of inspiring. Kristi works each day to be worthy of the gifts her class brings. She knows the world is going to be pretty amazing with kids like these in it. Finally, Kristi would like to thank her family: her sister and brother-in-law, Jen and John, for being cheerleaders a nation away, and her husband, Geoff. Geoff is the kind of man who bought the first Smarter Charts off Amazon.com, even though there were twenty copies in the house. He is kind, he is thoughtful, he is brilliant, and at every point she wanted to crumple, he helped her back up.

Introduction

Since finishing *Smarter Charts*, we have been amazed at the ways teachers have responded. We have gotten emails from schools as far away as Hong Kong about the ways charting has changed for teachers. We have heard that kids use the charts more, that teachers see more independence. Though we thank you for sharing your success stories, all the credit goes to you: the teachers who are willing to try and the vision they create for what is possible. And so we began asking ourselves, "What else is possible?" Where else could charting take us? And as always, the children and teachers we worked with showed us the way.

Figure 0.1 We are growing our brains!

Art teachers and music teachers in the schools we worked in asked: "Will this book help me and my charts?" Other teachers asked: "What about in science and social studies?" In some classrooms we visited, we saw daring teachers attempting to change how they were charting math and how they were using charts in areas other than literacy. As we started to dabble in a world less familiar to us, we got stumped. What *does* effective charting look like in math? Social studies? Science?

Figure 0.2 The door to an art room.

Charting Our Course: The Questions That Guide Our Process

As we started to think this through, we realized that as teachers ourselves, we did not have the strongest vision of what charts in the content area should look like. We had some thoughts, but we were in no way bursting with ideas. The relative lack of strong, engaging, thoughtful charts in the content areas makes sense in the context of recent surveys of teachers published in the *Report of the 2012 National Survey of Science and Mathematics Education* (2013) which showed that the majority of instructional time is spent on reading instruction (eighty-nine minutes) compared to fifty-four minutes per day on mathematics instruction, nineteen minutes per day on science instruction, and sixteen minutes per day on social studies instruction. When we do things infrequently, they will naturally be more difficult. In short, we were out of practice with teaching in the content areas and out of practice with charting what we taught.

We started to wonder if we could apply all we had learned about literacy charts from exploring brain research, design theory, and the world of advertising to all subject areas. Would the charts teachers found most helpful to literacy instruction and student independence be just as helpful in the other content areas? Could the way we used

Figure 0.3 A chart to support growth in writing.

charting to help clarify our teaching make the teaching happening in other subjects not only clearer, but more strategic? These nagging thoughts became the driving questions that helped us make some discoveries about charting that led us to write this book, *Smarter Charts for Math, Science, and Social Studies.*

What We Have Learned About Charting and Why This Book, Too

Since the writing of *Smarter Charts,* Kristi decided to return to the classroom after years spent working as a literacy consultant alongside Marjorie at the Teachers College Reading and Writing Project. She was happy to find a position in a school known for its commitment to thoughtful and responsive classroom practice, its intellectual and reflective staff, and its wise administration. A few weeks after being reintroduced to the wild lands known as teaching (kindergarten in particular), Kristi received her first bit of feedback from her principal. It was simple, and it was direct: "I can see all the thoughtful instruction happening in literacy from the charts on your walls. What is happening in math, social studies, and science? It is hard to tell what is happening in your teaching in those areas."

As far as feedback goes, it was dead-on. As Kristi stood and looked at her classroom, the walls near her writing and reading areas were bursting with kindergarten student work, co-created charts, and enlarged annotated pages of mentors that children used as inspiration. Along her math wall, lonely tumbleweeds blew in the barren land below the number line. Was she teaching math? Yes! Shapes and counting strategies and games galore! But where were the repertoire charts? The routine charts? The process charts? The charts that show vocabulary and the charts that show models of how thinking can look? And, looking around further, there were even fewer charts for social studies and science. Talk about a wake-up call!

In Marjorie's visits as a literacy consultant to schools across the world, she experienced a similar sense of disequilibrium when looking at the charts on classroom walls. Literacy charts were thriving, but oftentimes the only charts to support thinking in any given content area was a sample of a problem or a preprinted poster from a published program. At the chart workshops we presented, people started to ask: "How does this look in math? In social studies? In science? In art or music?" As we sat over coffee on a Sunday afternoon, we knew

Figure 0.4 A chair is its own chart in the music room.

that our work in literacy provided a map and a guideline to these un-"chart"-ed waters, and there was a need to venture forth. And so we began on the journey, which resulted in the book you hold in your hands. We found that when we developed charts to go with math and other content area instruction, some of the thinking we'd done around literacy charts matched this new work exactly. But we also experienced exciting new shifts in thinking and language as we struggled to develop effective, engaging, and empowering content area charts.

Charts Still Build Independence and Increase Cognitive Engagement

When Kristi teaches in small groups or one-on-one in reading and writing workshop, she dons a hat with red on one side and green on the other. When she is on "red," she is closed for business. This means that as Kristi is working with children in small groups and one-on-one, all the other children can use charts and partners for help with everything short of catching on fire. In short, the charts serve as a way to enable children to solve problems independently. When your mom teaches you a family recipe, you jot down notes so when you go to make it on your own you have support. We believe the same idea holds true with charts; charts provide reminders and examples of your teaching so that new learning is more easily replicated by students.

Figure 0.5 Kristi's "Closed for Business" hat.

Our chart work in literacy helped us (and helped the teachers we work with) empower children to make decisions independently while simultaneously teaching the language of reading and writing. Students could refer to charts that held strategies they were using to tackle areas of trouble. They could use charts to remind them of the steps in new processes they were working to make automatic. They could give suggestions to each other based on annotated mentors the class had studied. As we shifted our charting work into the content areas, we kept the same goal in mind: What do we need to make visible to help children be more independent, efficient, and flexible in their own learning?

No matter what area of the curriculum, we found that clear visuals, simple language, and constant reflection on charts, as we first outlined in *Smarter Charts*, were the key to helping children gain independence and agency in their learning. The more we charted, the less repeating we did and more teaching was possible. An uptick in the attention Kristi paid to her content area charting led to an uptick in the independence of her students—she now uses her red and green hat during math and other content area times as well!

The transfer of independence and engagement to the content areas was exciting to watch and experience, but it was not always an easy transition to move our thinking about literacy into other areas. We uncovered some tricky spots, and in doing so, grew more insights and ideas about charts and the teaching they represent.

A Chart by Any Other Name Would Smell as Sweet: Shifts in Chart Names

When Marjorie started thinking about this with teachers she works with, she flipped open to the field guide on the inside cover of *Smarter Charts* and started a discussion: What would each of these types of literacy charts look like in other subject areas? As she and the teachers struggled through the exercise, some new thinking was born.

In *Smarter Charts*, we referred to charts that outline the characteristics of a "genre" for children and called them (somewhat obviously) "genre charts." In math, social studies, science, and across the day, *genres* didn't feel like

Figure 0.6 Talking charts with colleagues.

the right word to describe concepts and types of information that children need to learn. Just as genre charts teach specific concepts, we found ourselves wishing for similar charts across the content areas—for example: squares have four corners, a key helps you read a map, an insect has an abdomen. After talking this out with friends and colleagues, we decided to rename genre charts (also somewhat obviously) "genre and concept charts." The concept chart is the cousin of the genre chart in that they both provide information about something specific to content.

As Kristi continued to make charts in her classroom, she drudged up another quagmire: What about charts that present multiple options, but don't really lay out detailed strategies? For example, once Kristi had taught a few math games she made a chart entitled: "When I Think I Am Done. . . ." Much like its related writing chart, this chart gave children options for what to do when they felt like they had completed their work on a math investigation. The options were: check my thinking; add more explaining in pictures and words; play a math game. This useful chart presented a list of choices, but it felt weird and inaccurate to classify this kind of chart as a "strategy chart." We determined that both these types of "option charts" and charts that laid out multiple strategies could be renamed "repertoire charts." These charts outline a repertoire or selection of skills, strategies, activities, and so on, that a child has access to and can choose based on needs and wants.

Kristi's experiences with a new teacher evaluation system based on Charlotte Danielson's work (2007) and Marjorie's work with teachers who were being evaluated drew our attention more fully to the importance of growth and feedback. We found ourselves creating and using rubrics more often. In literacy, whenever we showcased and annotated the best possible version of skills in context, we called it an "exemplar chart." As we created a diverse variety of rubrics (from math responses to science writing), we discovered that rubrics are actually just another form of exemplar chart. In our discussions of exemplars, you will also find a discussion of rubrics. Despite these shifts in names and expansion of their categories, it is still the thinking behind the teaching that leads to the success and quality of any chart.

Teaching Is Still a Process, Not a Program

Both Marjorie and Kristi have some dieters in their lives. Their friend, Tina, has been attempting to lose weight through a diet that gives her a day-by-day outline of what she can eat. One week she can only eat things that are green, for example, and another week she can only eat protein in the form of nuts and twigs, or something equally as complex and confusing. Tina has to stick by the program day by day, and if she skips something or binge eats the leftover cupcakes from a school party, she has to backtrack to day one. Tina is not losing much weight.

Their friend Fran, on the other hand, went to see a nutritionist. The nutritionist asked Fran to keep a food diary before their meeting. They met and talked over the diary, and the nutritionist asked questions like:

"What makes dieting tricky?" "What is your greatest food weakness?" "Do you work out?" Together Fran and the nutritionist developed some guidelines for her eating over the next few months, and Fran made follow-up appointments to discuss how the weight loss is going and look over her newest entries in the food diary.

Tina sees dieting as a program: something you do and then it is done. You do not change your life, your habits, or your choices. You do what the diet says until you lose weight, and then you are done with the diet. Fran sees dieting as a process: you learn how to eat healthy as you diet. It requires knowledge and interaction between the expert and the novice. One plan is not suitable for everyone given that each person is unique with habits and mind-sets that influence everything one does.

We believe that solid teaching is a process. Though you can use program materials, it will not work to follow a program one day after another without reflection, assessment, or responding to the unique students you teach. As Kristi worked through the math materials provided by her district, her math coach gave her this advice: "Start with the students and select what you need from the program." This same theory allows you to use this book regardless of the curriculum your district supports. You do not need to use the charts provided in your school's curricular materials if your students do not need them—rather, investigate what is tricky, teach (and chart) what students need, and reflect on the changes you see.

We do not purport to be experts in the teaching of math, science, social studies, music, or anything else for that matter. What we do have to offer is our ability to translate sometimes complex ideas into kid-friendly visuals and steps to make visual the abstract, to make simple the complex. We believe that thoughtful teachers, with charting tools at their fingertips, can create meaningful examples of visible learning that help children learn strategies, develop an understanding of processes, and refine their own thinking when problem solving and learning new materials.

We, and many of the teachers we work with, have found similar thinking pathways with the advent of the Common Core State Standards (CCSS). For the first time, these standards detail both content children need to know and skills children need to develop and internalize regardless of your district's program choices.

Charting and the Common Core State Standards

For the first time in our presenting lives, the one question we don't have to ask is: "What are your standards for this state?" The CCSS provide a common language and also a tool that is removed from the specifics of your program or school that we can use to talk about charts. So rather than referring to a specific program throughout this book (and thereby frustrating any teacher using something different), we will lean heavily on the CCSS for Math, Reading Informational Texts, and Speaking and Listening, as well as some early drafts for Social Studies and Science, as a way to think about charts that support students in different grades. As powerful as the standards are in helping teachers talk about skill development, developing teaching (and charts) to meet them illuminates an interesting issue.

When Kristi and her kindergarten colleagues mined these standards during common planning times, they happened across an interesting phenomena: When the standard named a skill, there were often multiple entry points to that skill. For example, in kindergarten the

CCSS in math say children will "understand addition as putting together and adding to." Any teacher of addition knows that teaching *one* way to add will not suffice for a classroom of thirty unique students. Underneath the idea of "understanding addition" are multiple techniques: drawing a picture, using manipulatives, writing the algorithm, counting on in one's head. It was through this work that Kristi came to understand the intersection of teaching as a process (What do *my* students understand about addition?) and the use of programs (Which *ways* will I teach my students to add, and thereby increase their understanding of addition?). At the crossroads is where charts emerge and become useful tools.

Career and college readiness is not limited to meeting academic standards alone; rather there are a host of character traits that enable children to be successful in academics, yes, but more importantly, in life: flexibility, persistence, and resilience to name a few. Charts help grow children as people and thinkers, too.

College- and Career-Ready Is a State of Mind

Many researchers, including Carol Dweck (2006) and Paul Tough (2012), have found that effort over intellect determines one's success in life. Charts, which make teaching visible, provide an implicit model of the fact that learning requires effort. Charts lay down pathways for children that say: Look, you can do this—just follow these steps!

Charts enable children to remain persistent and resilient in times of learning challenge. Repertoire charts provide multiple avenues to reach a goal, process charts give step-by-step instructions for difficult skills, and exemplar charts show examples of what can be achieved.

When teaching is never made visible and accessible, we communicate an unintentional message: If you don't get it this time, you will never get it. By teaching with charts, we say: This work is hard and will take practice, but here is a way to do it and it is right here whenever you need guidance.

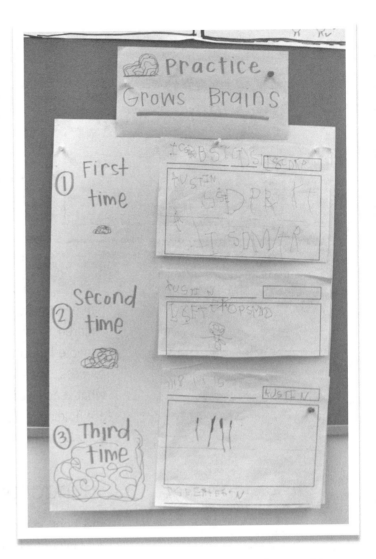

Figure 0.8 Teaching persistence.

Figure 0.9 The entrance to Kristi's classroom.

Christine Hertz, a third-grade teacher, related this story about the power of charts and persistence. As Christine talked to her class about growth mind-sets, she recorded ideas about what someone with a growth mind-set would say ("I can try again," "Let me think about how to do this better," "I can keep at this") on a chart so children could use the phrases to help them out of hard spots. Midway through a child interrupted her and said, "But don't *all* charts help us out of hard spots?"

From the mouths of babes, right? With each interaction and response, we began to realize that the power of literacy charting we had worked to name, harness, and articulate in *Smarter Charts* could also empower children to access every subject they needed to learn. This included expected routines, understanding of genres and concepts, concepts of process, strategic actions, and exemplars to use as models. Isn't that what teaching is all about? This was the inspiration for the book you are holding in your hands now, *Smarter Charts for Math, Science, and Social Studies.*

Foundations of Chart Making

This book stands on the shoulders of *Smarter Charts* and continues our dialogue on chart making, including our beliefs about teaching and learning and the questions that continue to guide our process. *Smarter Charts* provided the basics of effective charting: the language of charts (both words and visuals), when to make them, where to put them, how to get kids to use them, and ways to assess their effectiveness. This book assumes much of this knowledge in its references and implications, so we suggest you read that book first. For example, in the Introduction, we explained the research behind the charting such as educational pedagogy, design theory, brain research, and visual literacy, showing the ways this knowledge leads to improved memory and learning. In other words: why charts help learners learn. Then *Smarter Charts* teaches in depth three key aspects of effective charting:

- What do I put on my charts?
- How can I help my students use the charts independently?
- How do I assess the success of my charts?

The first section in *Smarter Charts* highlights the basics of language and visuals that help students read and recall the information being taught quickly and efficiently. The second section is all about when and how to make charts, where to put them, and how to make them memorable. And finally, the third section discusses ways to assess any chart's effectiveness and to get children to actively use the charts to become more independent problem solvers. If you are interested in diving into these ideas in detail, you'll find in-depth information in *Smarter Charts*.

A Note About the Ecosystem Surrounding This Work

With Kristi in her own classroom, and Marjorie working in scores of schools, we had a diverse playing field on which to test ideas. Each of these schools shared a few common traits that are important to identify:

- Workshop teaching: Most schools we work in teach everything (including math, social studies, and science) by first teaching a focused lesson lasting between five and fifteen minutes, then sending off children to pursue work independently, and then reconvening in a share at the end.

- Teaching in units: Units involve a way to group thinking together for children in an organized and sequential way. There is often a return to the concepts in the unit further along in the year.

- An emphasis on small-group work, independence, and agency: All the schools we work in emphasize a work time where children apply what they are learning in a project or activity of their choosing with support from a teacher or partners.

- Authentic instruction: The schools we work in rarely use worksheets—rather, they emphasize designing work that is more closely aligned to that of authentic mathematicians, scientists, and social scientists. For example, rather than fill in a worksheet about a leaf, children might gather leaves and record what they notice in a science or inquiry journal.

Though you do not need to have the same organizational structures in your classroom, it is helpful to know the conditions that existed to make this work possible. For more on workshop teaching, we would suggest you look into the groundbreaking work of Lucy Calkins, Donald Graves, and Math in The City Founder, Cathy Fosnot.

Figure 0.10 A busy workshop classroom.

Directions for the Reader

This book is organized differently from *Smarter Charts* in that each section focuses on one particular type of chart (routine, genre and concept, process, repertoire, and exemplar) and how it might be used across a variety of content areas. First we define the type of chart and explain its purpose—in other words, what it is and why you would make it. Then we describe how each chart is made and used, followed by a "Charts in Action" section that shows a real-life scenario using the chart with kids and includes lots of chart tips along the way. Another new addition to this book is our examples of how each type of chart might be used across several content areas, such as social studies, science, and math. In these sections, we also discuss the rationale behind the chart's use, choices that can be in the hands of children, and next steps. We also include a focused section called "Beyond the Basics" where you will find more research-based thoughts about charting.

Each section stands on its own so once you have read the book through to learn about each type of chart, you can return to any section based on your instructional needs. For example, if you are looking to see some possible ways to break down a strategy into clear steps, then you will turn directly to Section 3 on Process Charts, where you will find lots of helpful advice and many examples of actual charts that can act as mentor texts for your own charts. We know as teachers that sometimes all we want is a little inspiration to spark our thinking and to get us on the right track.

We are excited to share our newest thinking about charts with you here and hope to continue this charting conversation with you on our blog, Chartchums (www.chartchums.wordpress.com), and through our Twitter chats via @chartchums. Happy charting!

SECTION 1: Routine Charts

**Supporting the Engagement Necessary
for Independent Functioning**

What Is It? Why Would I Make It?

Each morning Marjorie wakes up, goes to the bathroom, then heads to the kitchen to make coffee. This is her daily routine and because it never changes she can do each step quickly while half asleep. When this routine is disrupted, like when the coffee tin is empty or the alarm doesn't go off, she must quickly make other choices. She must try something else, like boiling water for tea or skipping the coffee altogether to get out of the door so as not to be late for work. It is only when a routine is disrupted that you appreciate how smoothly routines can make your life go. See Figure 1.1.

In schools, routines have the same effect—they pave the way for the smooth functioning of each day, and they help lots of people work and move together, almost like a beautifully choreographed ballet. But this ballet does not just happen as a result of wishing and wanting it to happen. Every teacher knows that at the beginning of the year, routines must be planned and taught to establish an environment where all children can play and learn without too many disruptions. Our goal is for children to be able to run the classroom without us even being there!

Figure 1.1 Students study a writing routine chart to figure out what to do next in Valerie Geschwind's classroom.

In fact, planning ahead for the times we will not be there to control every movement and moment during a day is crucial. Think about what your students will need to know and be able to do to be productive, positive, and proud throughout each and every day. And think about possible charts that might make these expectations very clear to students and "guest teachers" alike.

When we teach procedures that lead the classroom community to operate smoothly so that tasks can be accomplished safely, expediently, and successfully, routine charts are the artifacts (and reminders) we leave behind. Routine charts show the foundational steps for doing something—steps that will reduce chaos and lead to a productive use of time so that more active learning can take place. When we wrote about routine charts in *Smarter Charts,* we said their purpose was to teach a routine or behavior to students. Routine charts are often numbered, written like a how-to, include photographs of students in action, and are most often made at the beginning of the year (2012, xxi). The ultimate goal of routine charts is for the behaviors they describe to become internalized so that eventually the charts are no longer needed. See Figure 1.2.

Most important in the creation of routine charts is that children play a role in establishing the routines they describe and they understand the purpose behind each one so that they choose to learn the procedures that will lead the classroom community to function without a hitch. They need to understand the "why" of each routine. This means having honest discussions with your students about why routines might be needed and when they should be put into place. In the book *Drive,* Daniel H. Pink's compelling book on motivation, he suggests that for routine tasks to be taken on by others willingly and well, we must put three key practices into place (2009, 62):

Figure 1.2 Returning books is something that needs support in the beginning of the year.

- Offer a rationale for why the task is necessary.

- Acknowledge that the task is boring.

- Allow people to complete the task their own way.

In elementary classrooms, the rationale for routine charts is often to reduce chaos and tears. And although most teachers resist using the *B* word (*boring,* sh!), acknowledging that a task is less than exciting shows empathy and helps the kids know we're on their side. Whenever we ask kids to do something, we must also remember to be open to their approximations and celebrate how they go about each task.

Routine tasks help with organization and efficiency when setting up and cleaning up. They help children navigate their way around the classroom, learning to use materials and tools with the least mess possible while ensuring safety. Routines teach life skills, showing children how to self-manage and work cooperatively with others. The following is a list of possible routines that might need to be explicitly taught:

- caring for materials
- organizing and planning
- working with others
- solving problems.

Charts take time to make, so when to make a chart and why to make it should be considered thoughtfully. Remember, a chart is not just a thing on the wall: It is an artifact of your teaching and a tool for students to use when learning a new challenge. For example, if you can simply *tell* your students, "Please go to the meeting area with your inquiry notebooks and reread what you last learned," and they all do it, then you won't need a lesson or a chart. However, if you want students to set up in a particular way that they have never done before—for example, bringing their inquiry notebooks and also rereading and reflecting by jotting follow-up questions or new wonderings they have—then you will probably need to model this new behavior. A chart can serve to reinforce your modeling and act as a reminder of these new expectations. When, after repeated practice going through the steps of this routine, you notice that no one seems to need the chart anymore, then you can retire it or make smaller versions to put into their notebooks as reminders should they ever forget. See Figure 1.3.

Figure 1.3 Routine charts can help children learn ways to calm their bodies when coming in from recess.

How Is It Made? How Is It Used?

Vocabulary and word choice are important considerations when planning for any lesson, especially those revolving around routines. If, for example, you want to teach your students how to handle such tasks as pouring and mixing, and you plan to use specific measurement terms like *milliliters* or *centimeters*, then you will want to preteach these terms so your students will understand the directions. Sometimes what seems to us to be the most obvious of routines is not so obvious to young children.

Kristi will never forget the time early in the year when she asked her new kindergartners to come to the rug for a minilesson. She was thrilled that they stopped what they were doing to head for the rug right away, but less thrilled with the way they ran as fast as they could and once there, just hovered around chattering like a flock of wild birds. She thought her words had been very clear, but she could see by the children's response that they'd been anything but. Her brand-new kindergartners did not know what a minilesson was, let alone how to get ready for it. Once she got them settled, she decided on the spot to create a chart, which broke down the steps into a simple, three-step how-to. The next day she photographed her students as they did each step and later added the photos to the chart. Kids of all ages love being the star of the show, or of the chart in this case. Classrooms of all ages may need support with these small routines that yield big organizational results. See Figure 1.4.

Figure 1.4 First-grade teacher Sarah Hang helps a student through the steps of coming to the rug.

Clarity: Planning the Succinct Steps in Your Chart Before You Teach the Routine

Many of our conversations about charts have been about making our teaching visible so our students understand and use what we are teaching. Developing student independence is a constant pursuit. In other words, charts are for the kids. Right? Of course, you might answer. Who else would they be for? Administration? Parents? Classroom visitors? Yes, yes, and yes. But after years of launching units, planning and delivering lessons, reflecting on what is working and what is not, we have come to realize that besides the students, the person the charts might be most helpful for is the teacher. Yes, the teacher. And this is why.

A teacher's plate is always overflowing with stuff to do, deadlines to meet, paperwork to complete. Weekends are spent planning lessons for the week ahead. It is enough to keep anyone's head spinning. So to keep from becoming dizzy, we suggest planning the chart simultaneously with planning your teaching, as a way to maintain focus and clarity. Start by asking yourself, "What might a chart look like that will help my kids know what I am trying to teach?" Thinking about the key characteristics of a good chart will make the planning process much easier and help with clarity and cohesion. See Figure 1.5.

Headings

The heading is key because it announces the big idea or goal of what you are teaching. It can be a question, a statement, or a reminder. Using strong verbs works to send the message that actions need to be taken. Trying out a few possible headings is a good way to check whether you have a clear goal in mind.

> "Looking to set up for math games quickly?"
>
> "This is the way a science experiment goes!"
>
> "Don't forget these three easy steps for taking care of pattern blocks!"

Language

Now, what words to use? Do you want to introduce certain academic vocabulary or use familiar words? Will you use these words in phrases, in sentences, or as labels? What are the reading levels of your students? Then consider how you plan to use the words. If you want to repeat these words over and over so that the children begin to chant them, then short phrases might be best. See Figure 1.6.

Visuals

We often put photographs or drawings up on our charts to give children a picture of what certain behaviors look like, such as sitting hip-to-hip or looking at your partner. Pictures offer children clear examples of the steps it takes to move from the table to the meeting area, or from the table to the door. These are the kinds of charts we often create during the first days of school.

Using charts as a planning tool, no matter what the subject, will help make planning simpler and more effective because it will help you, the teacher, focus and keep your main goals always in sight. See Figure 1.7.

Figure 1.5 Post-its are an easy way to jot down chart ideas in a plan book.

Figure 1.6 This second-grade pack-up chart uses more writing and more sophisticated vocabulary.

Figure 1.7 This chart for fire drills uses simple line drawings.

I'm Done!

Routine charts are needed throughout the year, but they are especially useful early on. "I'm done!" is a typical refrain during the first weeks of school whether children are reading social studies texts, playing a math game, or doing a science observation. Making clear the routine you expect students to follow can help diminish familiar outbursts such as these. For example: two children have finished playing a math game. They sit there for a moment, then begin chatting about what is for lunch or what they plan to do after school. They stop playing the game and don't seem prepared to do any further mathematics.

Teaching children what options they have when finished with the task at hand can allow both teacher and students to accomplish much more. "What do you do when you think you are done?" is a predictable question that will arise each and every year. Planning for possible suggestions and steps that will help each child become more independent is an invaluable aid in making the entire year go smoothly. Putting these suggestions and tips on a public chart will help remind children how they can help themselves when they come across dilemmas such as these and many more. Charts can help every child in your class to believe that they can help themselves solve any problem or answer any question they may have, not just today, but in life.

Beyond the Basics: Technology and Charts

Many teachers use technology, like SMART Boards and iPads, in their classrooms. Charting and technology intersect, but not always in the way people anticipate. The most effective charts are ones that rely less on teacher action and more on student interaction. See Figure 1.8. Charts kept on SMART Boards are usually selected and shown by the teacher; it can be cumbersome to move between charts or show multiple charts at once. For that reason, it makes sense to use technology to make charts in easier and more engaging ways and post them in places where children can independently access them. Some apps and programs that have proven their worth in improving charts are:

★ **iFontMaker:** Make and save your own font and drawings to use on any computer. This makes recreating charts in smaller sizes much less time-consuming.

★ **Pic Stitch:** Show pictures in sequence within one frame—especially helpful for routine charts.

★ **Snap:** Annotate photos before you print them. These make handy reminders for children.

★ **Qrafter:** Generate your own QR codes that children can access with an app.

Figure 1.8 Katie Lee teaches a routine for when kids feel "done" in math.

CHARTS IN ACTION: TEACHING THE WHOLE CLASS AN EFFICIENT WAY TO GET READY FOR MATH WORKSHOP

Some routines are osmotic, meaning they pass through the boundaries of subject unhampered by the change. Preparing for any kind of workshop learning is one such routine. Workshops have predictable structures: the class gathers for a focused short study, students go off to work independently or with partners, they return to share findings and thoughts with the group. Reading and writing are two subjects taught in a workshop structure, but so also are math, science, art, and others. This "getting ready" routine is being first taught in math, and then will be revisited in other applicable subjects throughout the day. Because of this, some of the chart language will seem vague, but remember this is happening in the context of teaching and demonstration. Although the chart and routine will travel from subject to subject, the teaching will show the specifics of each. This class has had math workshop for a few days and the "coming to the rug" aspect seems long and full of questions about where to go and what to do. After Kristi teaches the routine, she will then teach a math lesson and the class will have its regular math workshop.

Lesson Focus: Mathematicians prepare to learn by getting their materials ready and getting to the rug quickly every time.

Materials

- **Chart paper with the following heading: "Ready, Set, Work!"**
- **Four 8.5 × 11-inch sheets of different-colored paper (turned into sticky notes using a repositionable glue stick)**
  - **Blue paper, with "Folder and pen" written on it**
  - **Green paper, with "Get paper" written on it**
  - **Orange paper, with "Name and date" written on it**
  - **Yellow paper, with "Come to rug" written on it**
- **Student math folders in bins at the tables**
- **Pens at tables**
- **Paper in the math center**

Lesson

Kristi begins by gathering the whole class on the rug with no materials. She leans in to gather the attention of the children. ***"Friends, we have been in school for five days now and each day has been an adventure! We have been learning all sorts of fun things, but I have been noticing something a little worrisome."*** Here Kristi pauses and shakes her head in disbelief. *"Sometimes it takes so looooong to get ready that we don't have enough time for the really fun work! So today I am going to teach you a way that we can get ready quickly, which isn't the fun part, and instead have more time for all the things we have been doing like solving math mysteries and writing books—which are tons of fun!"* See Figure 1.9.

Chart Tips

- Remember to state the rationale.

- Use your body and voice to engage.

- Don't be afraid to acknowledge that routines can be boring.

Figure 1.9 Kristi settles the class on the rug to start.

Kristi points to the heading of the chart. *"This chart is called 'Ready, Set, Work'! Because getting ready is kind of like a game. As a matter of fact, you kind of read it like this: 'Ready, set . . .* **work!"**

Chart Tips

- A playful attitude is always going to work better.

- Be prepared for giggles, emphasize that part of the game is doing the steps correctly.

"Okay, there are two ways to start getting ready and I am going to show them both to you. You get to decide which you want to do first!" Kristi sticks up the blue paper ("Folder and pen") and then the green paper ("Get paper") side by side on the chart. Two kids immediately get up to do it and Kristi calls them back with a *"Not yet! Let's finish the chart first!"* She then taps the chart and says, *"You can start with getting your folder and pen and putting them at your table or you can start with getting your paper from the math center. You have to do both though. Let's read these two steps."* The class reads the words together and Kristi taps her head. *"Think which one you will do first."* See Figure 1.10.

Figure 1.10 The first two items go side by side.

Chart Tips

- Get children interacting with the chart.

- Since these two steps are interchangeable they are side by side and not numbered.

- Preparing the steps ahead of time makes this quick and easy.

"Okay next step!" Kristi puts up the orange paper that reads, "Name and date." She points to it and says: *"Read it with me."* The students do, and then she says, *"Once you have done that, come to the rug!"* and puts up the yellow paper. Each of the papers have simple line drawings as a reminder of what each step says. Kristi asks the students to reread the chart with her and as they read she adds arrows pointing down to show the flow of the steps. See Figure 1.11.

Chart Tips

- Color-coding helps children differentiate the steps.

- Color-coding allows for a light prompt: "Check the green one again!"

- Arrows can be a useful symbol.

- Note how much is co-constructed versus how much is prepared.

"Okay," Kristi says, *"Let's try this a few kids at a time. We will say the steps out loud as the kids do them, and we can tell them how they are doing. I will snap some pictures that can go on the chart later."* Kristi calls two rows to practice the

steps. The rest of the children read the steps as the "practicers" do them, and the class gives the practicers feedback about how they are doing. Kristi snaps photos on her cell phone to print later and then the students switch roles.

Figure 1.11 Adding the next step.

Chart Tips

- Photos will make this chart feel like it belongs to the students.

- Going in groups reduces traffic flow and also allows for multiple repetitions of hearing the routine.

Once everyone has had a chance to practice and to give feedback, and once the class is resettled on the rug, Kristi moves the chart to the back of the easel and begins her math lesson.

Chart Tip

- Keep the chart part active and fast so children can settle into the meat of the next lesson.

Next Steps

Practicing once does not provide enough time to learn or internalize something new. This lesson represents the *beginning* of learning a routine, but not the end. This routine will be repeated in reading and in writing, as well as math, over the course of a few weeks. Each time, you'll scale back on your prompting, and eventually an element of speed will be introduced ("Can you do it before the timer goes off?"). To help children learn the steps, this chart will be reread in shared reading and also put in the take-home notebooks children have for shared reading materials. The routine itself will also be subject to revision over time as needs change in the classroom. See Figure 1.12.

Figure 1.12 A student demonstrates getting paper.

CHARTS IN ACTION

Routine Charts Across the Content Areas

There are more similarities than differences among routine charts across different content areas because they all tend to deal with getting tasks done efficiently, with minimal disruption. They are all designed to encourage students to play active roles in the implementation of the routines they describe. Here we provide a few examples of the types of charts you might see in several different content areas, specifically social studies, math, and science. As you read, we suggest you focus your attention on the similarities to see how easily routines can cross-pollinate, creating a healthy, blooming classroom environment.

Social Studies Focus: Building and Caring for a Classroom Community

Rationale

A chart like the one in Figure 1.13 addresses the issues that come up when a community of people lives and works together. When speaking with children, you might point out that an organized cleanup will not only go faster, but will also make building the next day even easier, since it won't be hard to find the blocks one needs. Cleaning up *can* be as fun as playing, if it feels playful. Put on jaunty music, don hard hats, or whistle while you work. Before you introduce any routine, ask yourself, "What is the reason to do this?" Then explain the reason to children. A little bit of purpose can go a long way.

Decisions That Can Be in the Hands of Children

As mentioned previously, one thing that makes routines more motivating is choice. When building a routine (and its chart), consider what steps children will have choice in. In the previous example, it is choosing the blocks to start with when cleaning up. In a packing or unpacking routine, it could be the order children put things in (or take things out) of their backpacks. Not every mind works the same way, and leaving wiggle room for choice allows children to make sense of the routine in their own way. Remember Daniel Pink's suggestion to allow people to complete each task their own way? Of course, he was referring to adults in the workplace, but we can still provide our children with guided choices that allow them to develop independence.

Figure 1.13 A routine for cleanup.

Social Studies Routine Chart Possibilities

★ "Field Trip Behavior"

★ "Think, Pair, Share Routine"

★ "How to Make a Guest Speaker Feel Welcome"

Next Steps

Imagine what a cleanup chart for art, Legos, or math would look like. What is the rationale for doing it the way you envision it? What decisions can children make within the routine to keep them motivated and invested in it?

Math Focus: Playing Math Games

Rationale

Arguably, the most important part of math games is *playing*—and a chart like this minimizes the amount of time spent chasing down lost items and arguing over who goes first. When speaking to children you might emphasize that the game is the fun part, and having a routine helps them get to the fun all that much faster. See Figure 1.14.

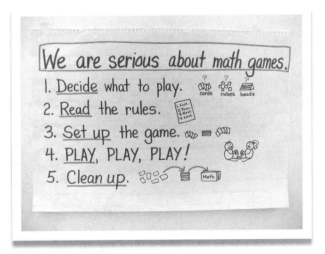

Figure 1.14 Routines for math games.

Decisions That Can Be in the Hands of Children

In terms of big problems for little children, deciding who goes first is a doozy. Teaching strategies for determining who goes first fairly can help ease this common classroom tension. Allowing for choice in the strategy helps children feel like the situation is fair and increases the chances of each child accepting the outcome. You can easily capture these ideas on a repertoire chart, which we talk about later in Section 4.

Next Steps

Think about other times where children need to interact successfully with each other and materials: science, reading, writing. What will that routine look like? Why should the routine go that way? What choice do the children have?

Math Routine Chart Possibilities

★ "Calculator Care"

★ "Linking Cubes Fix-Up (Unsticking and Putting Away)"

★ "What to Do When Interrupted"

Science Focus: Setting Materials Up for a Particular Procedure

Rationale

When Kristi cooks, there are many "I need *what?!*" moments midway through. At times, entire recipes have been tanked midcooking by missing ingredients that are nowhere in the house. Science experiments can have similar issues. Especially in science when timing is important, having materials on hand allows for a careful study of the results, instead of a midexperiment scramble. As Marjorie's seamstress mother and carpenter father used to always say to her, "Measure twice, cut once." Help children understand that careful preparation allows for better results. See Figure 1.15.

Figure 1.15 "Ready, Set, Experiment!"

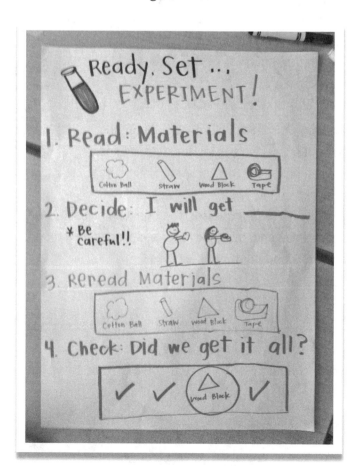

Decisions That Can Be in the Hands of Children

Depending on how you run science in your room, the children themselves may even be deciding which experiment to do. If not, and the whole class is studying the one concept, children can take ownership of who prepares what. If it feels faster to you to distribute supplies or prepare children in groups ahead of time, consider that teaching how to prepare for an experiment actually encompasses a bigger life skill: organization. There is value in doing the small tasks with as much care as the large ones.

Science Routine Chart Possibilities

★ "Scales Set-Up"

★ "Setting Up Your Notebook Entry"

★ "Returning Materials"

★ "Checking Out Books"

★ "Safety Routines"

Next Steps

Are there other times when children need to prepare for a particular procedure or activity? Is there a way this chart could work in other subjects with a few simple word changes? Reusing the same routines in different areas can reduce chart clutter and emphasize transference. Plus, repeated actions become second nature and go even faster when done across the day.

Common Core Connections

The science standards emphasize *doing* science over just telling kids about science and encouraging student inquiry so they make discoveries and experience those eureka moments most scientists and researchers live for. In other words, helping students become active thinkers and independent problem solvers in their pursuit of understanding; to learn how to work like real scientists and mathematicians do. If we want to hand over more responsibility to our students, then we need to make sure we teach them how to be, do, and act like authentic researchers in our classrooms.

Other Curricular Areas

It is not just elementary education teachers who make charts. Art teachers, music teachers, and gym teachers all have routines and expectations to keep their days flowing smoothly. See Figure 1.16.

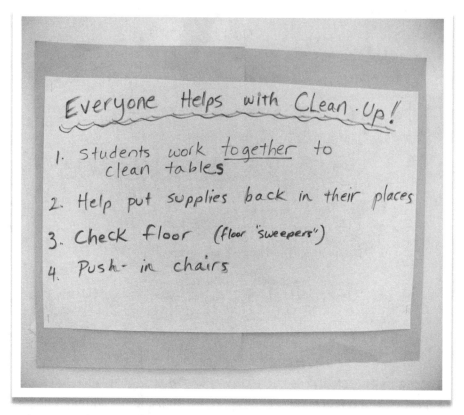

Figure 1.16 This art room chart lays the rules for community cleanup.

Other Curricular Areas

★ Art: "Art Studio Basics for the Handling and Care of Materials"

★ Music: "The Key to Harmony in Music Class"

★ Gym: "Body Be Aware in Gym and Everywhere!"

Last Words

Only when routines get disrupted do we truly realize their value. In thinking through the routines that the classroom needs and engaging children in their creation, enactment, and subsequent charting, we teach children the skill and value of organization. So often we organize things *for* children. Through charting, we can teach children how to organize *themselves* for success in school, at home, and in life.

Charts That Teach Beyond "Just the Facts"

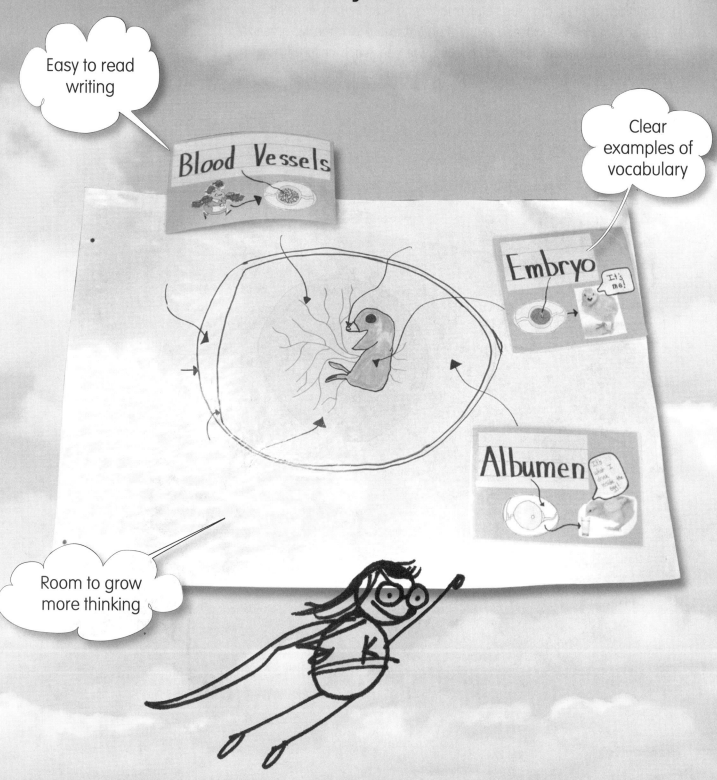

What Is It? Why Would I Make It?

When Kristi was growing up in the eighties, one evening ritual in her family was to watch *Dragnet* reruns on Nick at Night. Though this was not exactly fodder for forming friendships as a child, it implanted one phrase in her mind: "Just the facts, ma'am." Straight-laced Joe Friday voiced this line when witnesses veered off from the line of questioning. (Side-note: *ma'am* is, in fact, part of the quote, which gives a nice window into sixties' gender politics.) What does this have to do with genre and concept charts? Quite a bit, actually, since one of the main purposes of these charts is to record and exhibit the important concepts in a unit of instruction—that is, facts.

When we first spoke about these charts in *Smarter Charts* (2012, xxi), we called them "genre charts" because the information displayed was about a specific type of writing and reading, aka: *genre*. When we began to expand our charting work into other areas of the day, we realized that a chart that taught specific information was still needed, though "genre" seemed too narrow a title. In naming some of these charts "concept charts," we attempted to identify a very specific type of instruction: essentially, teaching (and the subsequent chart) that illustrates "just the facts" (or ideas and concepts, key vocabulary, dates, and other important information) in a unit. Note: Please take the word *facts* with a huge grain of salt. The world is rapidly changing and understandings are rarely black and white. Along with any fact, we are also teaching thinking skills, processes, and bigger connecting ideas that are at least as important as the facts, if not more so. See Figure 2.1.

In all curricula, a portion of the instruction is centered on vocabulary and concepts or ideas. Concept charts

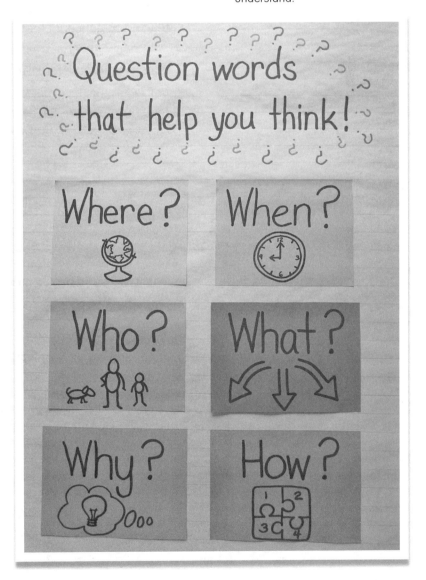

Figure 2.1 Question words are important concepts to understand.

capture and display this information for children to reference again and again in discussion, writing, and thinking.

In a geometry unit in math, for example, the names and characteristics of two-dimensional shapes will be taught and should be displayed so that children can refer to the shapes accurately throughout the unit. These are not strategies, a process, or anything other than information that the world possesses (that objects with no sides and angles are called circles or ovals) that you also want your students to possess.

Understanding these pieces of information allows children to negotiate their way through the world with a common language and shared understanding. Depending on your grade level (and often your city and state), the concept you teach will differ, though there will always be some overlap. There will, however, always be ideas and vocabulary that children need access to. Those things will be your responsibility to teach, and concept charts can help.

Concept charts are the charts most often included in prepackaged units, or available for sale at teacher stores across the country, so any teacher right now might be asking, "Why would I make it, when the textbook company made it for me?" Well, why make a meal when you can buy a frozen one from the store? When you cook for yourself, or

Teaching Vocabulary Through Concept Charts

Concept charts display important dates and names, and also, maybe even most importantly, vocabulary for children. The use of specific academic language is a critical facet of success in school. Domain-specific vocabulary is a key component of teaching any subject, but it is not just the naming of things that is important, it is developing an understanding of what these words mean in the context being used, and then using the words frequently and precisely when speaking and writing. In *Bringing Words to Life*, Beck et al. mention that a child needs eight to ten encounters with a word for the word to be learned (2002, 73). The Seeds of Science/Roots of Reading project (Cervetti et al. 2009) recommends that to truly learn vocabulary, students need to "do it, read it, write it, talk it," with the end result being that these words are used dozens of times across the course of any study.

your family, you make a million little choices that reflect what you and your family value: less salt, no peppers, extra garlic, lots of sauce, no sauce, and so on and so forth. Premade materials, much like packaged foods, are developed to an invisible norm and won't reflect your very visible range of students. They also don't deal with some of the nuances you may want to teach into. For example, a manufactured shapes chart might provide a ready-to-hang, clearly labeled, glossy, vibrant example of each shape you want your children to learn. But what happens if you have children who are still at a very concrete stage of development? They may not recognize a shape as a triangle because it is turned in a different direction or it is very narrow. Or they may think a square turned on its axle is a diamond, an entirely different shape. It is the teacher who knows her class and when multiple examples are needed. See Figure 2.2.

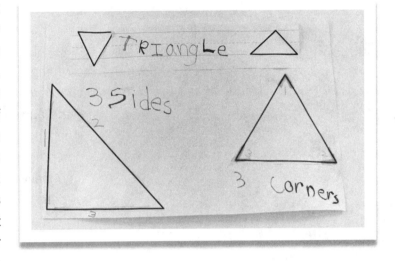

Figure 2.2 This chart was created with interactive writing, and there was much discussion around the many ways a triangle can look.

Though premade charts, like the ones you can find in a teacher store or accompanying a textbook, can serve as inspiration, one must always ask, "What does *this* class need to be successful?" Sometimes it means you need more, or sometimes it means you need less. In Kristi's kindergarten class last year, she only needed the rhombus and the square on the shape chart since those were the only two the children were not reliably distinguishing, but this year she needs the hexagon, rhombus, and trapezoid on the shape chart since these shapes are unfamiliar and pose a challenge for her students. Rather than swamp the chart with every shape, selecting a few critical ones allows for focus and usage on the trouble spots. You can't get that from a premade chart!

Charlotte Danielson, in her book *Enhancing Professional Practice*, compares the natural (and quite understandable) impulse of new teachers to stay close to the provided materials, but notes that skilled teachers whose teaching best matches students adapt, refine, and create their own resources (2007). Teaching in a flexible way, and therefore creating concept charts that reflect the diversity of prior knowledge and needed knowledge, is one way a teacher can demonstrate his skill in reaching a range of learners.

Additionally, the theory of learning by doing has been lauded as far back as Aristotle. He says: "For the things we have to learn before we can do them, we learn by doing them" (*Nicomachean Ethics*). When one co-creates a shape chart, drawing the red circle on the chart and then writing the word *circle* helps children learn the feel, the look, and the name *circle*. Danielson believes that a distinguished teacher's resources show "evidence of . . . student participation in selecting or adapting materials" (60). As we discussed in *Smarter Charts*, anything co-constructed will garner more attention and more usage than something just hung on the wall. If the purpose of charts is to help students become independent, we want to invest them in the construction process.

Finally, charts are never static, and that is true of concept charts as well. When we make or adapt charts, we show that learning is fluid and builds upon what we thought before. In revisiting and revising concept charts, we show children a visual of what is happening in their brains: Old information is revised and built upon, resulting in new understandings. See Figure 2.3.

Now that you are sold on the importance of creating or adapting concept charts with your students in mind, the next question becomes: "How do I decide which concepts to teach?"

Figure 2.3 In a small group, a child adds the word *long* to a chart on measurement words.

Identifying Concepts That Are Important to Teach

There are many ways to determine which concepts to teach students. Among them: conversations with colleagues, reflecting on past teaching experiences, assessments, studying state and local standards, and/or a close examination of materials. Whatever method you use, it must go through at least one lens: "What do my students need?" Let's look at one planning method in depth as we seek to answer that question. See Figures 2.4 and 2.5.

In *Understanding by Design*, McTighe and Wiggins start all unit planning with one big question: "What relevant goals (e.g., concept standards, course or program objectives, learning outcomes) will this design address?" (2005, 14). Regardless of whether you work from a social studies textbook or design your own inquiry studies, it's important to ask yourself that question.

To answer it, first gather all the materials you have around the unit—for illustrative purposes, let's imagine a communities unit in social studies for first grade. These materials might include:

- a textbook or teacher's guide
- read-alouds
- state or city social studies standards
- CCSS standards for reading informational texts
- big books or charts provided by the program.

Then, go through your material and make a list of several different things for your unit (e.g., Communities). We've used the NYC Scope and Sequence for Social Studies (2008–09) here:

- What vocabulary will children need? (According to the NYC Scope and Sequence, p. 5: first graders need to know: rules, laws, resources, symbols, monuments, services, direction and map words, etc.)

- What concepts will children need? (E.g., families are part of a community, symbols represent places, places in a community can be located on a map; NYC Scope and Sequence, p. 4.)

- What skills or strategies will children develop in this unit? (E.g., close study of photographs, map reading, drawing conclusions, interview and questioning techniques; NYC Scope and Sequence, p. 6.)

Next, decide which of this information should be taught directly and explicitly, and which of this information should be discovered over time through inquiry and study.

One way to think about this is: What information will students need to have to learn more? Certain vocabulary may be necessary to unlock keys of understanding. Also, consider what work will be meaningful to engage in for inquiry. It will not feel particularly useful for children to inquire into things that have simple yes-or-no answers. Think through what information they will need to know to inquire more deeply. In the example above, using symbols to represent places might be something children discover through an inquiry of maps, whereas the word *key* (as in *map key*) is essential information that is needed right away and won't be discovered through inquiry and close study.

Figure 2.4 Kathryn Cazes revises a concept chart with her students.

Figure 2.5 Conversations with colleagues can help you make decisions about which concepts and vocabulary to teach.

Skills, strategies, and routines will be charted in other ways (see sections on routine, process, repertoire, and exemplar charts), but vocabulary and concepts will ultimately end up on concept charts. To decide *which* vocabulary and *which* concepts, you might develop a quick formative assessment, for example: "Draw and label a picture of a community," or "Draw or write what you know about communities." From these assessments you can decide what will be critical new information for your students, taking care to think about what they know and what they need to know to be successful in their study.

Perhaps the most important thing to know about creating a concept chart is that it will not be static. As one progresses through a unit, learning becomes more specific and more refined. A concept chart with specific vocabulary will likely be revised when children gain more knowledge about the words.

How Is It Made? How Is It Used?

There are really two major times when information and ideas are introduced and clarified: at the beginning of a lesson, and at the end, depending on the method of instruction. For our intent and purpose, here are a few ways developed by the fine folks at the Reading and Writing Project (see the Units of Study in Writing [Calkins 2012]) to deliver specific information to students:

- **Minilecture:** A short (short!) delivery of information with visual supports. In geometry it might sound like this: "There are many different shapes that we see in the world. The shapes have special names and certain things about them that help us identify them. Let's look at some of them! This shape is called a *trapezoid*; what do you notice about it? That's true! It has four sides and four corners, but what makes a trapezoid special is how long the sides are . . ." (Teacher and students add to the chart as the lesson progresses.)

- **Read-aloud/video viewing:** A teacher-selected text or video that is going to primarily deliver information or ideas. The teacher may set this up by telling students specific things to look or listen for. In science it may sound like this: "Since we are getting to know more about sharks, we are going to listen for certain words in this book to see if we can figure out what they mean. I wrote them up in this chart for you, they are: *fin*, *cartilage*, *gill slits*, and *predator*." (Definitions go up at the end of the read-aloud after discussion.)

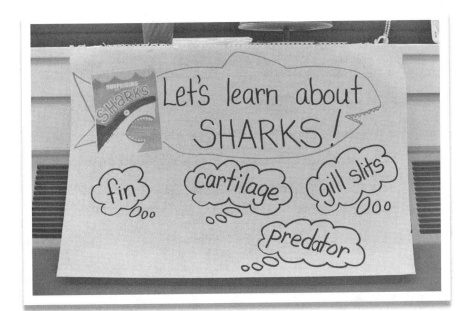

Figure 2.6 The thought bubbles emphasize that these words are important to listen for and understand.

Inquiry: After a period of study, children gather back with the teacher to discuss theories that have been confirmed or revised through their research. In social studies it may sound like this: "So we have been closely studying maps for a while now and we had some theories. We thought that the *M* signs might be where the subways are on the map, and the *H* might stand for hospital. Now that we have investigated this on our walk, what do we know for certain?" (Teacher and students add to the chart as they discuss.)

In each of these methods of delivery, the teacher is using her interactions with the students to guide what goes on the chart. As often as possible she starts with the language they use before guiding them toward more sophisticated understandings. See Figure 2.6. Many times this kind of chart has drawing or writing by the students on it—since they are the intended recipients of the knowledge, they are more invested if they've been involved in the chart's construction.

Once the chart is completed, it hangs in a place where students will be able to see it. Oftentimes the chart is brought to the rug during discussions so children will be able to reference the vocabulary or concepts discussed in it. It should be visible when children are writing and talking in smaller groups as well, since repeated usage helps understanding develop. See Figure 2.7.

Figure 2.7 This chart tracks children's thinking as it grows and changes through inquiry.

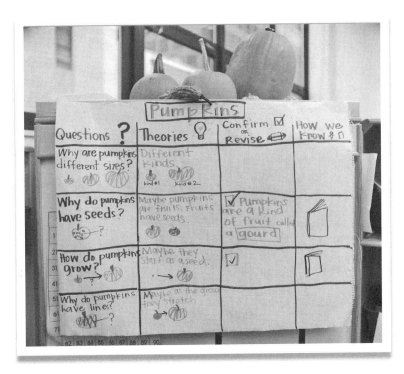

Beyond the Basics: Modeling a Growth Mind-Set Through Charting

Carol Dweck, author of *Mindset* (2006), writes throughout her book about the importance of effort over intellect. Children not only learn what we explicitly teach (the facts and concepts on charts like these, for example) but also our implicit models of learning and thinking. For this reason, it is important to revise and "grow" thinking in front of students. Charts that demonstrate development in thinking illustrate the importance of reflection and growth over a static product. Celebrate the messiness and change in thinking at the end of a unit to emphasize that it is not important where we started, but how we grew.

Most importantly, this chart is revisited and revised over time. If at first the students defined *gills* as "flaps that help a shark breathe," as the class continues to study, the understanding of how gills work will grow and the original definition will no longer be sufficient. Perhaps they will change the definition to say "flaps that help a shark breathe by taking the oxygen out of the water." As with all charts, this illustrates something greater than just the definition of gills; it demonstrates that thinkers never say they are done and that true understanding is a constantly morphing process. We live in a colorful world, and we do our students a disservice when we pretend things are black and white.

CHARTS IN ACTION: TEACHING A SMALL GROUP OF CHILDREN TO USE A CONCEPT CHART FOR TOPIC-SPECIFIC VOCABULARY

Since we are focusing on information and facts when studying content area subjects, charting the words being learned can be a great resource for students—that is, if they actually use the chart as a resource. In Section 3 of *Smarter Charts* (2012, 60), we wrote extensively on ways to encourage children to actively use the charts in the classroom to help them become independent problem solvers, reflective practitioners, and goal setters. This session builds on these beliefs and puts them into action by showing a group of second-grade children how to use the vocabulary that has been recorded on a concept chart and to put it to use to speak and discuss the topic at hand like experts or social science professors.

Marjorie had noticed that this particular group of children often spoke in generalities when talking about communities, saying things like, "If you live in a place that has lots of people, you are in a big place" instead of "If you live in an urban environment, you will be surrounded by lots of people." She had introduced this vocabulary over the past two weeks and had used the terms fairly often, but now wanted the children to use the words in conversation so they would truly learn them. She prepared small copies of the charts so that each student could point to the words they would use as they talked.

Lesson Focus: Social scientists use specific vocabulary to describe what they have observed about the world and what they are thinking so they can clearly teach others, like a professor does.

Materials

- **Chart created with students about ways to talk about communities**
- **Small copies of the chart, one for each student**
- **Highlighting tape**
- **Social studies notebooks**
- **Highlighting pens**

Marjorie begins the focus lesson:

"Good afternoon! I asked the four of you to gather round so you can talk about what you are learning about our community from our neighborhood walks, from the books we have read, and from some of the videos we have watched. But here's the thing. I don't want you to talk like second graders." The four sit up with eyes wide and look at each other with surprised expressions. *"I know you are second graders, but I think you are ready to start talking like the experts you are*

becoming, like social scientists, and you can do that by using the vocabulary we have been learning to talk and write about communities." See Figure 2.8.

Chart Tips

- Make sure the chart you plan to refer to is close by and accessible.

- You can either bring the kids to the chart or the chart to the kids.

- Photocopies of the charts make great artifacts to leave with students.

Figure 2.8 The chart ensures that the students will be successful in coming up with "professor" words.

Marjorie points to the chart "Ways We Can Talk About Communities" and continues. *"If you were giving a tour of our neighborhood community, like that big red bus we rode during our field trip to the city, and said something like, 'There are lots of people,' that would sound like a second grader—which makes sense, you are second graders! But if you wanted to use words that a professor of social science might use to be even more specific and clear, you could look at our chart here and choose some expert words to use."* Marjorie puts a finger on her chin and looks at the chart. *"Hmm, instead of saying, 'There are lots of people,' how could I be more specific? Hmm."* She touches the word *people*, then the line *How many?* then touches the words *population* and *density*.

Chart Tips

- Remember how important it is to teach children how to use a chart to help them do something better.

- The more a chart is touched, the more likely it will be used and become a helpful tool.

    "You can use the word *population*," Tiffany shouts excitedly.

    "Yeah, and *density* too," Jamie adds.

"Let me try that. Let me know if I sound more like a professor if I use those vocabulary words." Using a very serious tone, Marjorie says, *"'The population density surrounding the school is high.' Is that more specific?"*

"Yes!" the four all exclaim in unison.

"Wow! It's amazing the difference the words you choose can make in how you sound and how you think!" Marjorie looks again at the chart, then back to the children. *"Let's look at our chart again and think about which words are expert words that you could use to talk like a professor about communities."*

"Structures!" Cory calls out.

"Before you call out, really look at the chart and think about the words that will help you think and talk like a social scientist professor," Marjorie gently responds.

The children turn and look intently at the chart for a few moments, then Marjorie prompts them, *"Turn and talk about the words you think are really important to the subject of communities."*

Chart Tips

- Get the children to actively use the chart by prompting them to look and make decisions about what will help them most.

- Looking at a chart once is not enough. Prompt children to look again and again.

As the children erupt into talk, Marjorie leans in to listen, jotting the vocabulary she hears the children use and pointing to the chart. She then calls them back together.

"Okay, what vocabulary words would a social scientist use to talk about communities?"

"Population," Alyia and Jamie both shout out.

Marjorie turns to the children. *"Do you all agree that this is an important word to highlight on our chart?"* (See Figure 2.9.) They all nod

Figure 2.9 The colored tape highlights domain-specific words.

in agreement. Marjorie puts a piece of highlighting tape over the word *population* on the chart, then asks, **"What else?"**

Tiffany says seriously, **"Residential."**

"Come on up and help me highlight that important 'professor' word." Marjorie hands her a piece of the highlighting tape and helps her put it over the word *residential*.

The children continue to shout out words. **"Density!" "Urban!" "Structures!" "Suburban!" "Rural!" "Public!" "Communities!"** Marjorie highlights each one until Cory says, **"People!"** Putting her finger on her chin Marjorie looks at the word on the chart, and then turns back to the children. **"The word** people **is definitely one we will use when we talk about communities. Do you think we need a reminder to use this word or is this a word we use all the time already?"**

Tiffany's arm shoots up as she says, **"We know that word from first grade, so it's not a professor word."**

"Does anyone have a different opinion about this?" Marjorie looks around expectantly.

Jamie shrugs her shoulders. Alyia shakes her head, signaling *no*.

Returning to Cory, Marjorie asks, **"What do you think, Cory?"**

"I think we don't really need to put the tape on it 'cause we know that word already."

"Okay, so now that you have highlighted the 'professor' words a social scientist would use, you can try using them in a conversation about what you have learned about our neighborhood community. Pretend you are about to give a tour of the neighborhood community. Turn and talk, and as you talk, look up at the chart to help you get ideas about what you might say, and how you will say it, on the tour!"

Chart Tips

- The more you encourage students to interact with the chart, the more useful the chart becomes.
- Using highlighting pens or tape (or underlining, boxing, highlighting with a marker) is a way to revise a chart, which keeps any chart current and relevant.

As the children turn and start talking, Marjorie listens in, prompting as necessary. After a few minutes she calls them back together to recap and set them up for continued work in this area.

"So professors (and you really did sound like social scientist professors!), which words did you use to sound like a professor?"

Tiffany jumps up and points to the word *residential* on the chart. **"I used this word to talk about where my cousins live in New Jersey. They live in a residential neighborhood."** (See Figure 2.10.)

"Excellent! So from now on, try to talk like an expert by using expert words, and don't forget to use the charts and tools we create together to help you do this important work. I am going to give each of you a copy of the chart so you can remember the 'professor' words you will want to use when you talk and write about this topic. You can highlight the words you think are most important for you to remember to use whenever you talk or write about this topic."

Marjorie hands out the copies of the chart and gives the children some time to highlight the words using highlighting pens before calling them back together one last time.

Chart Tips

- Physically handing over the chart puts the responsibility right in the hands of the students.

- Having them mark up their own personal copies of the charts helps transfer the whole-class learning to individuals.

- Giving children their own copy of a chart and letting them mark it up gives them more ownership over their own learning. See Figure 2.11.

"Professors, you know what I am thinking? I am thinking that one thing that professors do is teach others to become experts in their field. Now that you

Figure 2.10 It is always a good sign when children use the chart as a reference.

Figure 2.11 Giving children their own copies of charts offers more opportunities for practice and hands over ownership.

CHARTS IN ACTION

are thinking and talking like experts, using the chart to help you, I think you are ready to teach the rest of the class to do this very same thing. You each have your chart where you highlighted the important words to use when talking and writing about your topic, so now would you each go to a table and teach the rest of the class some ways they can sound like social science professors, using the chart to help them remember the important words to use?"

"Cool!" Tiffany says, as the rest nod in agreement.

"Great! Let me stop the class and let them know that you will be coming to teach them something really cool and really important. Awesome work today!"

Chart Tips

- You really learn something when you have to teach someone else, so giving children their own copies of the chart that they can use to teach others reinforces what you have taught by giving it real purpose and importance.

- The whole class chart can be kept alive by sending it out into the world by your young designated emissaries.

Next Steps

This was one lesson, but a few more follow-up lessons will be necessary to get the children to use the domain-specific vocabulary more in their discussions and also in their writing about the subject being studied. By giving the children their own copies of the charts and then prompting them to use the charts in partnerships and small groups, you will be teaching the reason charts are created and ways they can be helpful. Too often children don't realize the charts are made for them, to help them as needed, and using them is not "cheating." At first it may sound a bit artificial because some children will just throw these words in anywhere, but with experience they will begin to develop an understanding of the nuances vocabulary knowledge allows. The vocabulary concept chart can also be revised to include some examples of how the words are used in conversations (transcripts) and in writing (student examples).

Genre/Concept Charts Across the Content Areas

Genre or concept charts help define whatever topic is being studied. For example, the charts often try to cluster information by categories and themes, or they list key elements. They are designed to help children recall key ideas as they continue to explore, experiment, and discuss to deepen conceptual understandings of the subjects being learned. These are the types of concept charts often seen in elementary classrooms, but are also the charts most often gathering dust because they are only referred to once, hung up, then forgotten. We offer here some reminders for how to make these charts pertinent, relevant, and useful.

Science Focus: Parts of a Plant

Rationale

This type of chart reinforces the vocabulary that is foundational to the learning of plant parts by combining words and pictures. The pictures are labeled or captioned with the children based on actual observations, photographs, or video clips. As with all genre or concept charts, children are encouraged to refer to the chart often to use the vocabulary being learned. See Figure 2.12.

Decisions That Can Be in the Hands of Children

Children can help decide which parts to draw first, what colors to use, what words to add during each step of developing this chart. Parts of the chart could be done during interactive writing or during the share time, which allows for student participation in the decision-making process as the chart is composed. Children can also be invited to revise the chart as more is learned or new information surfaces.

Next Steps

Plan to use this type of chart as a mentor text for students' science notebooks where you want to see headings, labeled diagrams, detailed pictures, and parts clearly delineated based on their observations.

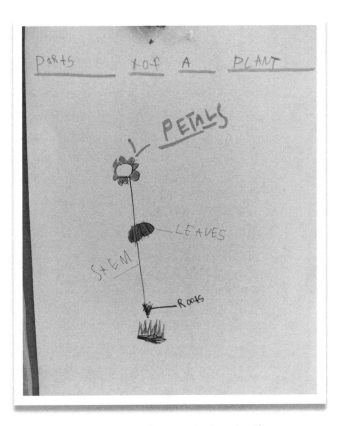

Figure 2.12 The scientific vocabulary was reinforced by creating this chart during interactive writing.

Figure 2.13 Two shape charts—one made with students, one made for students.

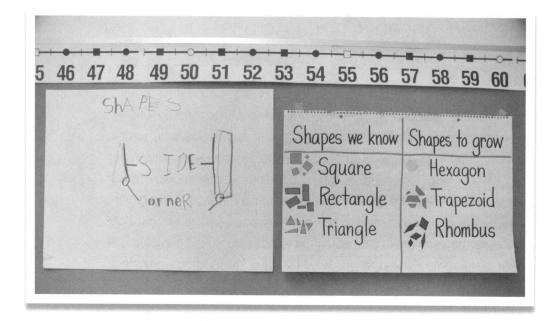

Math Focus: Geometric Shapes

Rationale

Geometric shapes are taught throughout the primary grades, so many children have some experience with their characteristics along with their names. But this does not mean students understand some of the nuances of shapes, for example, angles and congruence. Doing a preassessment to determine children's prior knowledge will help you determine what the children understand and know and what confuses them, and therefore what kind of information needs to be on the shapes chart in your classroom. A chart that simply lists all the shapes will quickly become wallpaper if many of the shapes are already known to most of your students. The idea of the chart is to push children beyond what they already know and into some new territory in a supportive way. See Figure 2.13.

Decisions That Can Be in the Hands of Children

Children can decide which shapes they want to learn more about or that they still have questions about. The children can't choose the colors of the shapes because these are usually aligned with the colors of the pattern blocks, but they can have input as to how many examples should be on the chart and even the size of the examples (small, medium, big or big, bigger, biggest). They can also contribute examples of things that contain the shapes on the chart ("A slice of pizza is shaped like a triangle!") and make drawings or find photos to add to the chart.

Next Steps

As with all genre and concept charts, how they are used determines their relevance and usefulness. Keep in mind the three *R*'s of charting: revise, reposition, or remove. Once a concept is learned, consider either revising the chart by adding in an additional complexity, such as more sophisticated vocabulary (e.g., *obtuse*) or by deleting words that have become automatic.

Social Studies Focus: Understanding and Asking Questions

Rationale

We use some words freely and often, not even considering whether the children understand what they mean. Sight words are one example. These words are chosen because of their frequency of usage in texts and their irregular spellings, but when some children continue to confuse words like *in* and *on*, we become puzzled. Making the words more visual is one solution; by simply drawing a square and writing the word *in* on the inside and then writing the word *on* on the top of the square, meaning becomes instantly clear. Once children are taught the meaning of these simple words, they no longer mix them up. See Figure 2.14.

Question words have particular impact in the content areas. Teachers and students alike often say question words together more as a phrase than as individual vocabulary words—*whowhatwherewhywhen*, or the 5 *W*'s—which has as much meaning as *lmnop* ("elomenopee") does to young children first learning the alphabet. Spending time on the meaning of each question word and what types of answers it elicits is time well spent. Three question words to start with are *who, where,* and *when* as they have fairly straightforward definitions and are especially useful in beginning inquiries. See Figure 2.15.

Decisions That Can Be in the Hands of Children

Once children have spent time exploring each of these question words for a week or so, they are ready to begin distinguishing one from the other as they talk, read, and write (in this case about social studies, but these words can be practiced in every subject area), and this is where the chart becomes a key touchstone. Each time children

Figure 2.14 Charts can help children picture what content words mean.

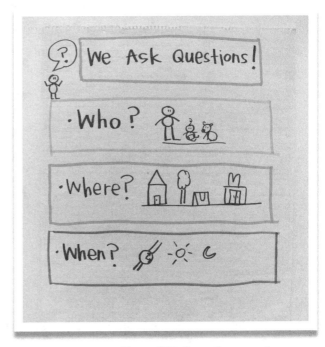

Figure 2.15 These three words are useful in beginning inquiries.

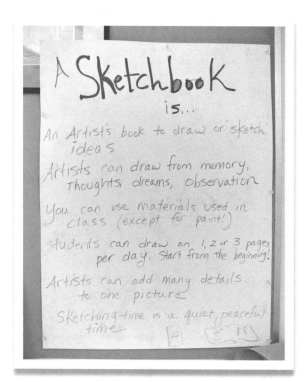

find they have asked a question using one of the words from the chart, they can look at the definition, then search for an answer that fits the meaning of the word. For example, if the child's question is "Who keeps the streets clean?" he might say, "Since *who* is a person, the answer to my question is going to be a person, so I am going to read looking for the name of a person who cleans the streets." For a *when* question, the child will look at what time or how soon something happens. This work is not as obvious as it may seem and well worth the time spent making sure each of our students understand what these words mean and how to use them correctly. See Figure 2.16.

Figure 2.16 This co-constructed art room chart captures the many possibilities of a sketchbook.

Next Steps

This chart will probably stay up for awhile in your classroom, adding the other question words one at a time, and pointed to often during discussions across the day. Then you might make multiple small versions to add to children's various folders where they are expected to use questions, like reading, writing, science, social studies, and math.

Other Curricular Areas

Throughout elementary school, children are learning and using new vocabulary and concepts. In art, music, physical education, and more, children are growing new thinking and new ideas. See Figure 2.17.

Figure 2.17 This music room chart explores the origins of musical styles and has plenty of room to grow as the students learn more.

Other Curricular Areas

★ Art: "Forms of Art"

★ Music: "Take Note of Musical Notes"

★ Gym: "Equipment You Need to Play Soccer"

Last Words

Genre and concept charts are tools meant to encourage understanding and use of important genres and concepts children need to learn in school and in life. But simply slapping up a ready-made poster filled with academic vocabulary (as shiny and colorful as it may be) misses one key element: time. Words should be added one or two at a time, and then children need time to inquire into where each word is found, how it is used, and what it might mean. Then they need time to use the word over and over again in discussions and in writing. The teacher's role is not to test but to teach—demonstrating, clarifying confusions, and opening up new questions for children to explore and develop. Genre and concept charts then become a lot more than "Just the facts, ma'am, just the facts."

Every Strategy Has a Process Attached to It

Heading states the goal

Uses symbols that are known

Concept broken into small, numbered steps

Built with students in mind

Be STRATEGIC

1. Think

2. Plan

3. Do

What Is It? Why Would I Make It?

In every curriculum and every classroom, there are moments where we find ourselves trying to understand how we will teach something complicated to the small children in front of us. When we realize the outcome we desire requires multiple steps in a specific order, what we have identified is a process that needs to be taught. In other words, a *process* is a series of actions or steps taken to achieve a desired outcome. This could also be the definition of teaching. Each teacher puts a lot of thought into how to break down the steps involved no matter what she is teaching. The "what" a teacher is teaching is often referred to as a *skill*. The "how" is usually referred to as a *strategy*—and for each strategy, there is a process, a series of steps.

A process is something everyone or everything goes through to get somewhere, to achieve a goal. Just consider something you learned to do recently. At first, each step probably felt laborious and complicated and you had to continually reference the steps to make sure you were on the correct track. Kristi experienced this with her dreams of making homemade pasta. Her first few attempts took hours as she looked between her recipe, YouTube videos, and her own cementlike dough. The process to complete a step, read the next step, try it, and repeat, at the end there was a bowl of slightly misshapen rigatoni to enjoy. With repeated attempts, she got the feel for making pasta dough, and now, happily for her family and friends, has found a process that works for her. It has now become a skill. She knows the steps of the process and the consistency of dough to the point where it is no longer a conscious thought.

Process charts take complex skills and present them in bite-size steps until children gain familiarity and fluency with the process. For example, when children are first learning to subtract, a process chart can picture and name each action a child can try as they proceed toward a solution. First, start with the bigger number. Second, take the smaller number and count that amount back. Last, look at what is left over. This chart will then be expanded to include other strategies for subtracting and eventually abandoned in favor of a new skill whose complexity demands a new step-by-step explanation. In this section, we will take a tour of some of the more common processes taught and charted in the primary grades.

Have you ever taught something that involves steps, and some of those steps seem to constantly be forgotten? Do you find yourself explaining something in a step-by-step fashion, emphasizing the order?

Beyond the Basics: A Close Look at the Word *Strategy*

The teaching of strategies is something every teacher does no matter what the subject, but there are a few different ideas about what the word *strategy* means in the world of education. The word is often used synonymously with the word *skill,* so to differentiate between the two we looked to several sources for clarification. The *New Oxford American Dictionary* defines *strategy* as "a plan of action designed to achieve a major or overall aim." Plan of actions (or strategies) can vary, but the aim (or skill) is stable and singular, a goal to be reached. In *Strategies That Work* (2nd Edition), Stephanie Harvey and Anne Goudvis describe strategies as something readers use to make sense of what they read and to use these strategies "flexibly, seamlessly, and independently" (2007, 21). Peter Afflerbach and colleagues define *strategy* as "deliberate, goal-directed actions" used when a skill is not automatic. In other words, "strategies compensate when usual skills fail" (2008, 369). Skills are automatic and fluent once mastered.

Do you catch yourself saying things like: "This is really complicated, how will I help them remember this?" Then you, dear teacher, probably need a process chart.

Process charts set up microsteps in a specific, rarely changing order. When children need to learn the steps in order, charting promotes consistency and accuracy on each attempt. Some things, like writing findings in science, may not need to be done in an exact sequence; you could draw first, or you could write first. Others, like hypothesizing before experimenting, do. In those cases, you will want to make a process chart. Not every step-by-step process needs a chart. Some are simple and easy to remember, but when the task is complex and something that children will be doing often, a chart is the best way to preserve that teaching.

Like all things charted, once you have identified the sequence and made it visible, it provides a scaffold for children to learn the process and internalize it over time by progressing through it the same way again and again. Ironically, the reason you would create a process chart is so that you will never need it again! This chart makes a successful process visible for replication by the students, and once it has been internalized, the chart becomes redundant and is retired from the classroom.

To better understand the way conscious focus on a process recedes into the background through practice (and the way process charts, which are initially crucial, are outgrown as students become adept at and internalize the process the charts describe), think of something that was once quite challenging for you that you now do effortlessly. For Kristi's kindergarten students, putting on a jacket is no easy feat. Arms can be turned inside out, you can spin in circles trying to find the other arm, you may get through both arms only to discover the coat is inside out (or upside down, or help us—both), and don't even get started on the zipper! This was once true for all of us, and most children (Kristi included) went through the process of laying a jacket upside down on the ground, inserting both arms, and flipping the coat over the head. See Figure 3.1.

Such a process begins with step-by-step instruction, "Now put both arms inside," and slowly becomes an independent skill for people around the world. This technique for putting on a coat takes step-by-step instruction for children to understand and use it reliably. At first, a teacher may help the child set up the coat and get her arms in, then will move to just oral reminders of the steps, until the child just does it. Eventually you move from the flip technique to the regular ol' one-arm-at-a-time strategy without a thought. What was once a very conscious step-by-step process is now something most people do without thinking about it. Earlier when we spoke of routines, the goal was to cut down on ambiguity and uncertainty, to make tasks automatic. These are skills, just like putting on a coat, making pasta, or tying your shoes. But the same process may not work for every child, so you will need to use your knowledge of each child to guide you—and you will undoubtedly discover more than one process that helps students achieve the same goal. We talk about this in depth in the next section on repertoire charts.

Figure 3.1 A process chart helps students remember each step along the way.

How Is It Made? How Is It Used?

Like all charts, the most successful process charts are made with students. Process charts are usually made in one day, and subsequent days will be spent practicing the use of the process, referring to the chart when one gets stuck or needs a reminder on what to do next. For this reason, process charts also make great minicharts, as different children may need different steps or different processes as they move forward in their learning progression. Malcolm Gladwell, in his book *Outliers* (2011), suggests it takes ten thousand hours to master something, so these are charts that will live in the classroom for a month or more, remaining in place, or with small revisions, even when the content changes.

Since process charts refer to a series of actions in a row, they are often made through acting out or closely studying the process. In the primary grades, a common standard for the first part of the year is understanding the rules of a community. In many classrooms, this is where a discussion of rules begin, and for Kristi where she began to teach a very specific process for settling disputes. Kristi had several children role-play problems and solutions with her in slow motion to point out key moments. Explicitly naming each part of the process helps children identify it and replicate it later. After a few rounds of studying problems and solutions, the class constructed the chart in Figure 3.2.

Beyond the Basics: Teaching Pro-Social Skills

A great resource for breaking social skills down into processes is *Skill Streaming the Elementary School Child* (McGinnis 2011). In it, there are step-by-step processes for:

★ asking for help

★ accepting no

★ listening

★ taking turns

★ asking to play

When a problem would occur (roughly every thirty seconds in September), Kristi would bring the children to the problem-solving center (where the chart now hung) to support their movement through the process. The class would also role-play problems, using the chart to move through the steps. Soon the children were identifying when they had a problem and would head to the problem-solving center unprompted. Kristi erupted with joy every time a group of children went near the chart. She knew that the message that kids can solve their own problems was received when she heard from a parent that one student had set up the same chart at home. Late in the year, the problem-solving center fell into disuse as children automatized the process and solved problems wherever and whenever they occurred.

This technique (one might even call it a *process*), of studying a process, charting it, and practicing it over time until the chart is no longer needed, is one of the best ways to make a process chart, regardless of grade or content area.

Identifying the Learning Process, and Then Charting It

"But," you might say, "what is a science process? A math process? A choice time process?" In the content areas, teachers are sometimes left to fend for themselves to determine the steps of a process. Marjorie was once reading a math curriculum that gave a list of ways to solve subtraction problems, including "count back." At first glance this seemed easy enough until Marjorie prepared to teach her students to do it. What was the first step? Put up the number of fingers to subtract? Should she put one number in her head and start counting back for the next number on her fingers or say all the numbers on her fingers?

Only when Marjorie tried to think of how to demonstrate it did she realize there were distinct steps, and teaching these steps explicitly would be useful for students to learn the process. Oftentimes this is how a process chart comes into being, through a teacher's repeated practice attempts at the skill, noticing each time she begins a new step. Just saying, "You count back by . . . you know . . . counting back" will not help children understand and replicate the process as they go

Figure 3.2 First, the scope of the problem is determined, then the actions.

Figure 3.3 Mollie Gaffney Smith teaches how to count back, step-by-step.

forward. So Marjorie began to count back giving herself a practice problem 12 – 5.

At first, she thought the first step would be, "Put twelve in your head," but that is only true in *this* problem, so she reworded it to: "Put the bigger number in your head." So far so good. Now this is where it gets tricky. Marjorie automatically put up five fingers, but how could she explain that to her mathematicians? So was born step two: "Look at the second number. Put up that many fingers." Marjorie now saw step three clearly, "Say the bigger number out loud and count down by one on each finger." That lead to the last step: "The last number you say is your answer!" Of course, she then tried it out with various other numbers to make sure the steps worked each and every time. See Figure 3.3.

So what should you do to develop a process in any area? Try to use the skill yourself. For example, in science, it might be creating an experiment; in social studies, it may be comparing and contrasting; in gym, it might be the proper way to do a push-up. The skill has probably become automatic for you, so at first the steps will seem elusive. It can help to give yourself a harder example than the one you are teaching your students. Then, reason out loud what you are doing and record the steps. Most importantly, check to make sure the steps work for the problem you are giving your students!

CHARTS IN ACTION: SUPPORTING SMALL GROUPS AS THEY OBSERVE AND RECORD IN SCIENCE

The reasons one creates a process chart are the same reasons a chart is often revisited: It is teaching something tricky with multiple steps where order *matters*. It is like learning a dance routine, where you have to spin before you kick or you will be kicking your spinning neighbor. Teachers often coach small groups through the order of a challenging process, gradually reducing the prompts so children begin to move through the steps independently. The following lesson follows one small group that is having difficulty remembering each step of an observation process; oftentimes they glance at the object and draw the whole thing without close study of what they are trying to represent. While this small group is meeting, the rest of the class is in science centers studying life cycles.

Lesson Focus: Scientists help themselves look deeply and notice more by tracking their way through the observation process.

Materials

- **Science folders/notebooks**
- **Small copies of the chart laminated or in sheet protectors**
- **Dry erase markers**
- **3-D models of butterflies (for observation)** (See Figure 3.4.)

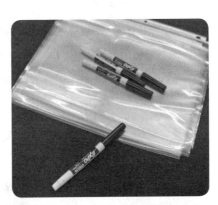

Figure 3.4 Gathering materials ahead of time is key.

"Jacob, Paloma, and Natalie, please come to the rug with your science notebooks and something to write with," Valerie begins. As the students settle in front of her, Valerie takes out the small laminated copies of the charts and says, *"We have been studying how much information scientists can get just by looking and we have this helpful chart to remind us of each step of how to look deeply. I thought we could study this a little closer and practice looking deeply at some butterfly models I have."* See Figure 3.5. The children murmur excitedly. Valerie holds one small chart and points to the title. *"We called this chart: 'To Look Deeply, Scientists . . .'"* The children chime in as she reads. *"Let's go through*

Figure 3.5 The teacher begins by pointing to each step illustrated on the chart.

the steps together." Valerie and the children read each step, pantomiming gestures for each one. A big circle with their hands for looking at the whole object, holding a pretend magnifying glass and closing one eye for looking at one part closely, tapping their heads for asking questions, and writing with a pretend pen for jot and write. *"Now remember, once you jot and write, the arrow goes around again to show you can look closely at another part."* See Figure 3.6.

Figure 3.6 The teacher coaches the children to use the tools introduced.

Chart Tips

- Have children look at the same chart with you (rather than their own small copies) at this point to ensure they are following along.

- Make the gestures match the visuals on the chart.

- Gesturing makes the steps more memorable.

- Have the small chart replicate the big chart exactly by taking a photo and printing it out on 8.5 × 11-inch paper.

- Sheet protectors or stapling acetate over the front makes for easy lamination.

Valerie hands out the small charts, as well as the dry erase markers, and says, *"This is a lot to remember but each step is important, so I gave you some tools to help you."* She picked up a dry erase marker and the small chart. *"Once I do each step, I can put a little check by it and look at the next thing I have to do. Does that make sense?"* All three children nod, eyeing the dry erase markers excitedly. Valerie sets up the butterfly models and says, *"Check your chart, what is the first thing to do?"*

Paloma says, **"Look at the *whole* thing,"** making the same big circle with her hand.

"Great, get to it!" Valerie replies.

Chart Tips

- Interactive charts are more likely to be used since they require a relationship between the student and the chart.

- When in doubt, break out the dry erase pens—they heighten engagement one million percent.

- Get the students practicing with the tool as quickly as possible.

As the children talk to each other about some of the things they are seeing, Valerie gently nudges the group, *"Once you have looked at the whole object, you can put a check by that and . . ."* As she lets her voice trail off, Natalie jumps in and says, **"Then look at one part real close!"** The children make the check on the chart and then look again. See Figure 3.7.

"I am looking at the feet," Paloma says.

Jacob, quiet until this point says, **"I bet these are the eyeballs,"** pointing to the top of the antennae.

Valerie, more concerned with practicing the process than nailing down every piece of content at this moment, gives a thoughtful face in response, saying, *"So you are looking closely at that part and wondering, 'What does it do?'"*

Valerie then says to the group, *"When you are ready for the next step, check off this one and check what you need to do next."*

Jacob checks it off and then looks at the next step. **"Draw and jot,"** he announces.

Valerie notices Natalie gazing into space and taps the chart. Natalie checks off the step and moves to draw and jot. Jacob then announces, **"I'm done."**

Valerie leans over to tap on the arrow and looks at Jacob. He stares at her, confused, and Valerie prompts, *"The arrow means to keep going around the circle."*

Chart Tips

- Using fewer words in your teaching is preferable; you want children to use the tool (not you) for support.
- Use symbols that are known (like arrows) to get the most out of children's sizeable visual literacy.

Valerie watches and coaches as the children move through the process once more, checking off on the chart as they go.

"Scientists, I am going to stop you so you can go back to your other observation centers. Before you go, let's talk about what we did here today."

Figure 3.7 The children mark each step as they progress through the process.

CHARTS IN ACTION

Figure 3.8 Children interact with the chart as they move through the process of looking more deeply as scientists.

Natalie jumps in, **"We looked at butter-flies!"** Jacob and Paloma nod in agreement.

"That's true," Valerie says. *"We also practiced with our chart."* Valerie holds it up.

Jacob adds in, **"Yeah, and we got to do the dry erase markers."**

Valerie nods and says, *"Anytime you have a big job and it's hard to remember what you need to do next, you can do what we did today, take a marker and check off what you have down and what you need to do next."* Valerie places the dry erase pens inside each sheet protector with the chart and says, *"You lucky ducks get to use this today, and every day when you need a reminder of your steps. Now off you go!"* She hands each one off to the children and they go to rejoin the class at centers already in progress. See Figure 3.8.

Next Steps

Valerie will closely monitor the students' work to see if she notices a change in what they are producing now that they have a better grasp on the process of looking closely. She may find that she needs to meet with the group again, since a process is not internalized overnight. It is possible that this will be a skill that the whole class will benefit from—tracking their way through a process—in which case, small copies might go on everyone's science notebook with a Post-it arrow that they can move. This process chart is not unit-specific; these students will observe in every unit in science this year. That is why the process of divining information through observation, a skill they will use in writing, reading, social studies, math, and life, is more important than the content at these moments (Jacob will learn that the antennae are not eyeballs over the course of the life cycle unit). Also tucked in to this work is a way to organize yourself as you move through a complicated process, something adults do now when they check off the steps when they assemble IKEA furniture or make a recipe for the first time.

Process Charts Across the Content Areas

Most everything in the world has a series of steps to help one do it. A process chart, like all charts, needs to start first with the students that you teach. In studying how children make sense of problems, you can develop a process that begins where they are and ends where you need your students to be. Each process chart suggested here shares similar attributes: They are numbered, break difficult concepts into small steps, and are built with students in mind, no matter the content area.

Social Studies Focus: Comparing and Contrasting Two Photos

Rationale

The ability to compare and contrast is an integral part of the CCSS for Informational Reading. Before beginning to compare and contrast texts and ideas, it can be helpful to teach children to compare and contrast photos. Visuals are much more concrete for young children and provide an entry point for this multistep process. Photographs can be found on photo sites on the Internet or taken on class trips. Looking at photos in this way builds a habit of comparing and contrasting that will stay with children throughout their lives. See Figure 3.9.

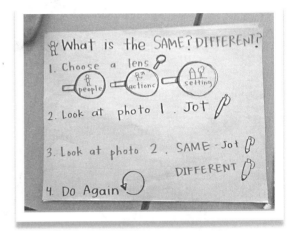

Figure 3.9 A chart to compare and contrast photographs.

Decisions That Can Be in the Hands of Children

Children need to be able to personalize a process to make meaning of it. Process charts often have choices built in that allow children to think independently about their own steps. In this case, children can choose the lens through which they look at the photos and the way

Social Studies Process Chart Possibilities

★ "Developing a Theory"
★ "Taking Notes When Reading"
★ "Figuring Out an Unknown Word"
★ "Determining the Main Idea"

Figure 3.10 A simple scientific process chart.

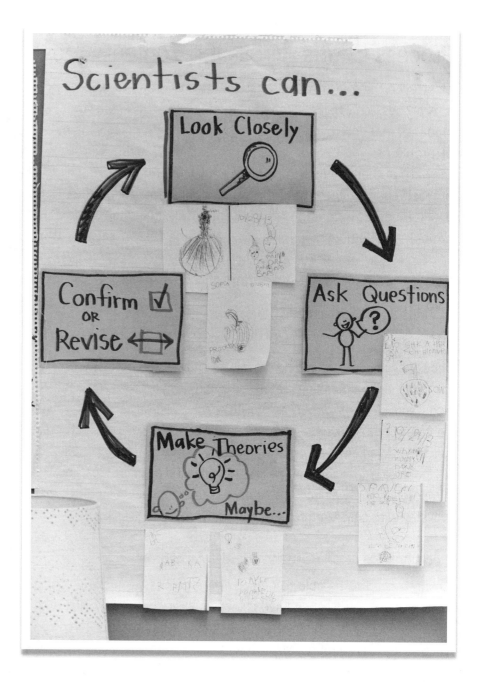

they record their thinking. Only the barest steps are required: Decide what you are looking at first, then look at one photo, then the next. The rest is up to the child. See Figure 3.10.

Next Steps

The next step in comparing and contrasting is not just noticing the similarities and differences, but using that information to help get ideas about what you are looking at. Developing an idea (theory, hypothesis) may have its own process chart as children begin to experiment with this complex skill.

Science Focus: A Scientific Method

Rationale

Note that the title of the chart in Figure 3.11 is not "The Scientific Method" but rather *"Scientists Can . . ."* Children learn from what we teach explicitly and what choices we make implicitly. Indicating that this is a method versus the only method allows children to see flexibility in the process. There is not just one way to gain answers—the chart offers one method among many. Having said that, it is important to teach children a process that helps them know how to proceed when they encounter a question. Investigating before experimenting is crucial to help children avoid reinventing the wheel. In addition, arrows show that any good investigation leads to new questions to explore. It is never ending. Teachers can always make the choice to replicate experiments to help children make sense of the results, but true experimentation means the answer is not simply available on page 42 of a textbook.

Decisions That Can Be in the Hands of Children

Children make many choices throughout this scientific process. The question is not dictated, nor is the source material from which they may investigate. Students will design the experiment and make choices in how to record what they notice. What is unchanging, however, is the order in which those choices are made—using this process, one makes a hypothesis before experimenting, regardless of experiment.

Next Steps

Each of the steps of this process may require further teaching and charting. Finding sources to investigate and reading those sources critically will be instrumental in forming a reasonable hypothesis.

Science Process Chart Possibilities

★ "Using a Measuring Cup"

★ "Creating a Hypothesis"

★ "Analyzing an Experiment"

Communicating what you have learned will be another area that will require additional teaching—there are myriad ways a student can teach others their discoveries.

Math Focus: Double-Digit Addition

Rationale

Double-digit addition is a big leap for many young mathematicians and they can become scared off by the big numbers in front of them. Teaching several explicit strategies for solving such problems lessens as shown in Figure 3.11, the panic and builds confidence that no problem is too big to be solved once you have the tools and a few different ways to approach such problems. In the CCSS under Mathematical Practice,

Figure 3.11 The steps for one way to add double-digit numbers.

Math Process Chart Possibilities

- ★ "How to Estimate"
- ★ "Steps to Solve Word Problems"
- ★ "How to Check Your Work"
- ★ "How to Measure an Object"

$$20 - 5 =$$
$$15 + 5 =$$

the first item on the list is "Make sense of problems and persevere in solving them" (MP1). Other goals include "Use appropriate tools strategically" (MP5) and "Attend to precision" (MP6). This process chart sets one possible model for the organization and thinking work required for adding two double-digit numbers in a way that underscores the connection between counting and addition by showing how base ten blocks can be used to break the numbers down into tens and ones and then regroup them at the end. Such a chart provides children with a starting point and illustrates that communicating the process is as important as the solution.

Decisions That Can Be in the Hands of Children

In this process, the thinking work: "*How* should I add together these two numbers?" is firmly in the hands of the student. Telling a child, "Build the first number" takes away the mental heavy lifting of mathematical reasoning. Allowing children to use tools like the base ten blocks

Other Curricular Areas

Clearly stated steps aid memory and leads to successful practice.

- ★ Art: "The Steps for Printing a Linoleum Block Print"
- ★ Music: "How to Warm Up Using the Scales"
- ★ Gym: "The Rules for Playing Tag"

helps them to visualize the double-digit numbers, while also providing something concrete to check for accuracy. The process helps children organize their counting, without taking the thinking work away.

Next Steps

Once children understand how to manipulate two-digit numbers into tens and ones using tangible objects, then there will be other processes taught for adding together double-digit numbers that will continue to build upon children's growing number sense. Then the process charts together can be used to teach children how to use the method that makes sense and is most efficient depending on the circumstances. See Figure 3.12.

Figure 3.12 Everything has a process.

Last Words

Sometimes, when Kristi wants to complain about overly complicated situations, she will say, "Why is this *such* a process?" The truth, however, is that life is built of a billion processes. As adults, many of these have become as second nature as breathing. There was a time, though, when everything from brushing teeth to approaching a math problem was novel and complex. For that reason, we create process charts, to ease the burden of memory on the mind and to provide a concrete and useful tool for children. As these processes become internalized through repeated use and experience, we collect them for children in a different way, as repertoire charts. More on that in the next section.

Decision Making and Strategic Thinking

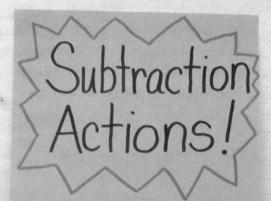

Catchy heading that grabs attention

Clear and concise language

Each strategy clearly distinguished

Visual reinforcement of the meaning of the words

What Is It? Why Would I Make It?

Marjorie was recently making spaghetti for her family when she realized the top was stuck on the jar of tomato sauce. Like all self-respecting chefs, she was prepared for such an emergency with a variety of approaches. First, she went to the sink to run hot water over the area where the lid met the jar. Faced with a hot but still stuck lid, Marjorie went for the rubbery potholder, placed it on the lid and turned with all her might. No closer to opening the jar than she had been before, Marjorie relied on the ol' tap-the-lid-with-the-back-of-a-knife trick. When she turned it again, a rewarding *pop* was heard and the meal was saved.

Marjorie was using a stockpile of techniques or strategies to achieve a desired result. When we teach children multiple ways to accomplish something (like getting the top off a jar of tomato sauce), we are teaching a repertoire of strategies; when we record that teaching and make it visible, we are making repertoire charts. Repertoire charts have a desired skill, goal, or behavior as a heading, below which possible strategies to achieve that outcome are listed. In *Smarter Charts*, we referred to these charts as "or" charts because one could do one strategy or the other to meet the goal. This flexibility and choice in repertoire charts distinguishes them from process charts.

How Is It Made? How Is It Used?

Teachers most often make repertoire charts to support children when there are multiple strategies, or options, to achieve one goal. Repertoire charts can ensure agency and success while offering options and choice, which leads to what Alfie Kohn, in *What to Look for in a Classroom,* calls "intellectual autonomy" (1998, 255). They provide children with options to try when a skill is not yet automatic. It is these choices that are often put up on charts as reminders of the deliberate actions students can take when something gets in the way of understanding or accomplishing something.

Repertoire charts are probably the most critical type of chart you will create with your students. Why? Because they send the message that learning new things is not automatic and there are multiple ways to approach any task. To use a repertoire chart successfully, we must teach students to develop an awareness of when something is not quite right and the can-do attitude that will allow them to try and try again, using the repertoire of options this type of chart provides.

Figure 4.1 This chart reminds children that there are several ways to take some space when a conflict has occurred.

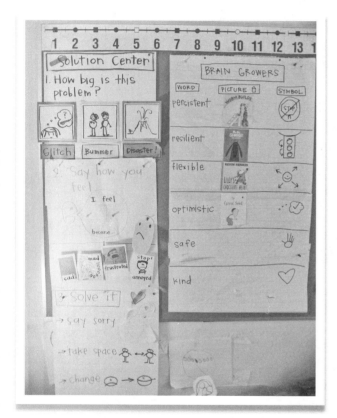

In Kristi's kindergarten classroom, solving a social problem with a peer is far from automatic. Though a process was outlined for solving problems in the previous section on process charts, Kristi found that her children needed more strategies. One solution cannot solve all problems, despite how much five-year-olds love the word *sorry*. The last strategy Kristi wanted children to rely on was coming to her for help, because the *last* message she wanted to send was "*You* need *me!*" so she elaborated on the problem-solving process chart by creating a new repertoire chart that included different options, all devised by the students themselves during classroom conversations. The repertoire of options for solving problems included:

- Say you're sorry.
- Take space.
- Change.*
- Get a teacher to help (or another problem solver in the room who would mediate).

The repertoire chart reminds students of problem-solving options that will help them develop a skill, but that alone is not enough. We also need to teach kids how, when, and why these strategies are useful and effective. In other words, we need to teach students how to identify why there is a problem, to think about a variety of ways to fix the problem, and to choose which strategy (or strategies) will be the most effective. And, with most problems, the first attempt at a solution does not always work or turn out to be the most efficient one, so we also need to teach flexibility and persistence when using the tools in the repertoire. See Figure 4.1.

Repertoire Charts Emphasize Flexibility, Persistence, and Strategic Thinking

Repertoire charts provide a scaffold that helps children develop flexibility and persistence. Rather than offering one way to do something, a repertoire chart captures the idea that there are multiple ways to achieve a goal. There is a reason "If at first you don't succeed, try, try again" is a maxim oft heard early in life. It is one that leads to success

---

*The word *change* serves here as a shorthand for the many discussions the class has had about ways one can make a change that will affect the outcome of a conflict. When students read the word *change* on the chart, they know that the word represents the idea of making a change in location, in materials, in context, and so on.

Beyond the Basics: Becoming Proficient in Skills

As children repeat the selection and execution of their repertoire for a skill, they move toward proficiency in that skill. In *Toward a Theory of Instruction*, Jerome Bruner wrote extensively and eloquently on the subject and believed that "learning and problem solving depended upon the exploration of alternatives" (1966, 43). He developed three conditions for these exploratory behaviors: activation, maintenance, and direction. When you are confronted with an issue for which you do not have an immediate answer, activation begins. The learner begins searching for possible alternatives to resolve the issue. Efficient and effective options are used again and again and therefore maintained. Maintenance supports what you have going, and direction ensures you remain on the right track to resolve the issue. We can assist in this process by teaching children how to make smart decisions about choosing from their repertoire.

later and one you can use when looking at a repertoire chart. McKinsey, a well-respected consulting firm, teaches its employees that when confronted with a problem, they can try something, *anything*. Even if an attempt doesn't work, its very wrongness will lead you toward the right path. In fact, Paul Tough, author of *How Children Succeed* (2012), makes the point that effort rather than intellect determines future success in life. Using a repertoire chart requires effort on the part of the learner: choosing a strategy or option, using it, reflecting on the success, and trying another one if needed.

The goal of repertoire charts is to send a clear message to each and every student that they have a responsibility to be active problem solvers by figuring out their own solutions. A big part of this is to also teach your young students how to make decisions about which strategy to use, when to use it, and why they would choose one tactic over another one. Consider the previous example—when and why might it work better to take space from a friend over talking it out? Giving students the skill and experience to be able to answer this question requires a lot more than simply hanging up a chart in a prime spot in the classroom. The chart is meant to be a living, breathing tool that is accessed often, revised as needed, and actively discussed and used by all. Once students practice choosing between strategies, or attempting another strategy if the first one fails, they will internalize not only the strategies but also the habits of persistence and flexibility.

CHARTS IN ACTION: USING A REPERTOIRE CHART TO MAKE A THOUGHTFUL DECISION

Once the last strategy has been added to a chart, it is easy to start thinking about the next strategies and the next chart. However, to really help students move into deeper strategic and extended thinking, it is critical to spend a few days teaching children how to sift through the repertoire of strategies they now know and make a decision about which one they want to use. In teaching, it may not be asking, "What's next?" but maybe "How can we better do what we now know?" that will enable students to become more successful independently. The following lesson looks at helping children select from four math strategies they have already learned and used to solve an open-ended story problem in the most efficient way possible.

Lesson Focus: When mathematicians have a problem to solve, they first think about all the possible ways to solve it and then choose the one way that works best for them and the problem.

Materials

- **Student math folders**
- **Large chart paper with the following problem: "Connor has five star wars figures. He wants to put them on two shelves. How many different ways could Connor put them on the shelf?" (Skill—decomposition of the number 5, CCSS Kindergarten Mathematics)**
- **Small copies of the math problem for each child**
- **A Post-it with each child's name on it**
- **Chart, "Ways to Solve Problems"**

"Over the past two weeks, we have worked really hard at trying different strategies to solve problems in math." Kristi taps the chart as she says this, and then continues. *"Go knee to knee with a neighbor and say what strategies you have been trying. You can use the chart to help you name them all."* Kristi circulates, listening to children name and explain the different problem-solving techniques that they have used.

Chart Tips

- Location matters; bring the chart to the children so they can see it easily.
- Touching the chart will draw more eyes to it. See Figure 4.2.
- Have children refer to the chart so they remember and use the academic vocabulary on it.

Rachel says, **"I draw pictures to do it."**

Figure 4.2 The more a chart is touched, the more effective it becomes.

Her partner Paloma nods and says, **"Yeah and sometimes I act it out too."** Kristi nudges them to check the chart and see what other ways the class has explored to solve problems.

Kristi heads back to the easel and gets the attention of the whole group again, ***"One, two, three, and back to me!"*** Once all of the heads have swiveled back to Kristi, she continues. ***"I hear many of you naming your favorite strategy to solve problems. Today I want to teach you that mathematicians don't just solve problems the same way every time. Sometimes they step back, study the chart and ask, 'Which way will help me solve this problem best?'"***

Chart Tips

- Repeated use of the chart will help children recall its contents.
- Explicitly naming that part of the problem-solving process involves close study of the chart.

Kristi reads the problem aloud: ***"Connor has five Star Wars figures. He wants to put them on two shelves. How many different ways could Connor put them on the shelves?"*** Kristi grabs a pen, acting as though she is about ready to work, and then says, ***"Wait a minute, wait a minute! I was just going to draw a picture, because that's my favorite strategy, but that may not be the best way to solve it. Let me step back and study this chart and really think about which of these might help me solve the problem best."*** Kristi taps her head in an imitation of the icon for "think" that is on the chart. ***"Hmm,"*** she said, ***"I already know about draw a picture."*** Kristi pantomimes drawing a picture in the air. ***"So let me look at the other ones . . ."*** Kristi names the other strategies out loud, mimicking the gestures that are represented by icons on the chart. She swipes her finger in a T shape for "make a table" and says,

"Make a table, that one might work for me here. It says how many ways in the problem, so I know I might have lots of answers. That would be a lot of pictures to draw, but maybe a table would help me." She moves on to guess and check, shrugging her shoulders and making a check mark with her finger. *"Guess and check, well maybe I could do that, I could guess how many ways and then see if it is true, but I could also act it out,"* Kristi says as she gives a dramatic flourish with her hands. (See Figure 4.3.) *"I could use manipulatives to be the figures and I could draw lines to be the shelves . . ."* Kristi lets her voice trail off and turns to the class, *"You know, I really need to think about which one way I am going to choose! Friends, can you study this chart with your partners and think about the strategy that will best help you solve this problem?"*

Figure 4.3 The use of dramatic gestures reinforces the point.

Chart Tips

- Match your gestures to the icons on the chart (and vice versa).
- Exaggerate your use of the chart to emphasize its importance.

Kristi checks in with a few partnerships of students. She pauses for a moment with Lucas and Ari, who are sitting in silence. *"What are you thinking?"* She asks.

Ari says, **"We are going to act it out."** Lucas nods.

Kristi asks, *"How did you decide on that one?"*

Lucas and Ari look at her for a moment, then Lucas says, **"Well usually I draw it, but I don't think I could draw all that, but if I just act it out then I can write down everything I do and that will be easier than drawing."** Ari nods in agreement and Kristi nods along.

She then gathers the attention of the class. *"Friends, the important work you just did was not finding the answer, but figuring out how to find the answer. Before you start any problem, you want to look at the chart to see what your options are, then choose one that will work for you and go for it! Right now, I am going to call you by rows and have you put your name next to the strategy you decided on."* As the children put their names up, Kristi has the teacher helpers distribute the folders and problem of the day. See Figure 4.4.

Chart Tips

- Use the chart as a way to keep children accountable—placing their name next to the strategy ensures they will try their strategy.

- Take a quick photo of the chart or jot which kids select which strategy so you will have a record to look back at.

Figure 4.4 One child puts his name on the strategy he thinks will help him most.

Next Steps

The goal of this kind of teaching is to develop thoughtful and flexible problem solvers. At the end of the math workshop, it will be helpful to have children share whether or not their chosen strategy was an effective and efficient way to solve the problem. Over the next week or so, you may repeat the idea that mathematicians don't use a one-size-fits-all theory when solving problems; instead, they thoughtfully consider their options and then go on to solve the problem. Revision of the chart might be necessary as children discover certain strategies work better for certain problems. If you notice children tied to a particular strategy, you may hold a small group to help these students become more flexible. These problem-solving techniques will not change substantially between grades, but the sophistication of the problems will increase. Developing a child's ability to be flexible and thoughtful problem solvers will be as critical as understanding that two plus two always equals four. See Figure 4.5.

Figure 4.5 Children's interactions with the chart keep it alive.

CHARTS IN ACTION

Repertoire Charts Across the Content Areas

Social Studies Focus: Places to Get More Information When Researching

Rationale

Figure 4.6 This chart shows a repertoire of information sources.

Oftentimes in content area teaching, the main sources of information are the teacher and the textbook. One way to empower children to become active learners is to teach them ways to gather information from sources beyond the teacher and the textbook. Hand in hand with this teaching will go teaching around being a critical evaluator of information from these sources. Most importantly, the purpose of this chart is to provide a repertoire of ways that children can take charge of their own learning lives. See Figure 4.6.

Decisions That Can Be in the Hands of Children

Children may already have a sense of where they can gather more knowledge about their interests. Possibilities that may not occur to you may be on the tip of their tongues. Children have access to a whole world of technology: blogs, websites, and apps that are designed to teach information. Even certain video games can be instructional and a source of information for children! When building a repertoire chart with children, remind yourself they are not empty vessels. Begin the chart with what they know, and add on what you need them to know.

Next Steps

Any of these options for seeking information will need to be taught: preparing for interviews, dealing with contradictory information, and getting information from texts that are too hard to read. Additionally,

---

Social Studies Repertoire Chart Possibilities

★ "Ways to Study Photographs"

★ "Ways to Develop Theories"

★ "Ways to Grow Your Thinking"

★ "Ways to Observe Closely"

you may find your list of ways to gather information is revised as children gain knowledge of additional resources in the world. As we discussed in the concept charts chapter, it is important to remember that it does no one favors to pretend the world is black and white when it is really multicolored.

Science Focus: Ways to Study Photographs

Rationale

When teaching the glorious work of science, we balance the work of experimentation with close study—often of photographs. Why? Photographs capture beautiful, surprising, rich, and unusual details that are often not accessible in our day-to-day lives. See Figure 4.7. Photographs can show an ant zoomed in one hundred times, or a hurricane as seen from above. Photographs add layers and textures of information to what we experience in our own lives. Photographs can

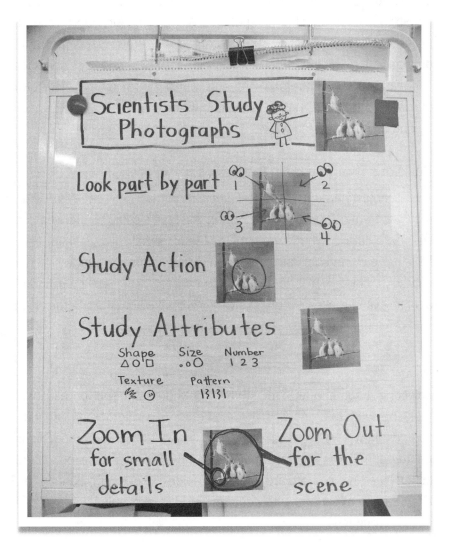

Figure 4.7 Observing for specifics can lead to richer understanding and thinking.

Science Repertoire Chart Possibilities

★ "Ways to Develop Theories"

★ "Ways to Grow Your Thinking"

★ "Types of Science Writing"

★ "Creating a Hypothesis"

★ "Questions Scientists Ask Themselves"

prompt questions for further study or theories to questions that have been lingering. Occasionally a child will study the photo as it comes around, but often photos are glanced at and passed on quickly. True seeing, like any other skill, requires attention—and can be taught. Helping children develop a repertoire of "lenses" (no pun intended) helps focus their eyes on the photographs in new ways, and thus deepens their thinking about what they see. Observing for specifics can lead to richer understanding and thinking. Providing a repertoire of ways to look at images is essential since each image will have unique elements to study.

Decisions That Can Be in the Hands of Children

The vocabulary around the different lenses will be more powerful when it comes from children. Asking, "When you look closely so that you can see more details, what should we call that move?" allows children to have more ownership, and then more independence, around using the chart. Attaching words to ideas helps children articulate their under-standings and makes it more likely they will take action using the chart as a reminder.

Next Steps

Selecting a suitable lens for studying a photograph will be essential teaching with this chart. If the elements in a photograph are tiny, zooming in will be a critical part of gathering more information. If the photograph shows a shark jumping out of the water, a close look at the action clues in the photo are the key to unlocking deeper meaning. This chart can be expanded with additional details explaining when to use each viewing lens.

Math Focus: Counting Strategies

Rationale

As children develop rudimentary counting skills, they often use disorganized ways of numbering objects and remembering quantities. This makes sense—young children are trying to remember the counting sequence and to attach that sequence to a pile of objects while simultaneously remembering which ones they counted and which ones they still need to count. Oy! Teaching strategies to organize counting helps children move toward automaticity with this skill.

Decisions That Can Be in the Hands of Children

Naming these counting strategies after the children who demonstrate them (e.g., "Finn's way") can sometimes help children more easily remember how it is done. Giving children the option of calling it "Finn's way," or "touch and say" gives them a way to name the technique in a meaningful way. Drawing pictures on these charts can be in the hands of children, supplemented with photographs that illustrate the work being done. See Figure 4.8.

Figure 4.8 The names attached to strategies give children a way to name the techniques in a meaningful way.

Math Repertoire Chart Possibilities

★ "Solving Number Problems"

★ "When I Am Done I Can ..."

★ "Addition Strategies"

★ "Subtraction Strategies"

Figure 4.9 Children engaged in discussions become metacognitive.

Next Steps

As children shed less efficient strategies, the chart should be revised to reflect their growing knowledge. For example, "make groups" can be further developed into "make groups of two, four, and ten," and "touch and say" may be revised to "touch and skip-count" as students are ready for this new strategy. The options on a repertoire chart should grow with your students and with your expectations for more sophistication and efficiency.

Last Words

When children become metacognitive (that is, they think about their thinking), we know that they are well on their way to being successful students. See Figure 4.9 above. When students can identify a goal and thoughtfully reflect on and select from choices, they have taken an active role in their learning. Having discussions around which strategies are most efficient and effective will lead children to increased reasoning skills and the ability to defend their process, which supports the recent emphasis on the "practices" of disciplines in math, social studies, and science. Repertoire charts are also tools that support children (and teachers) to move past a model of students as passive receptacles of information and toward a vision of children as active, engaged, and energized learners. See Figure 4.10.

Other Curricular Areas

Every subject has a topic, goal, or habit that comes with a repertoire.

★ Art: "Revising Your Project"
★ Music: "Ways to Change a Song"
★ Gym: "Choices for Warm-Up"

Figure 4.10 Children have a few strategies they can try for cooling down after gym or recess.

Bringing It Back to the Big Picture

What Is It? Why Would I Make It?

Kristi and her husband, Geoff, like to take on a complicated jigsaw puzzle every winter. Last year's entry was an image of the edges of fifty vinyl record sleeves. Geoff, an avid collector of vinyl records, quickly and easily found pieces that went together, using his store of knowledge about the names of bands and album titles. Kristi, less familiar with record sleeves, kept the cover of the puzzle box by her side so she could get a sense of what pieces went together and their general placement within the puzzle. For children, exemplar charts are like the puzzle box. When students don't yet have the vision or experience to create something, they need a visual that shows them how it can look. Geoff had expertise in records and could assemble album names from a mess of pieces in front of him. Kristi, the novice, needed the visual scaffold of the finished product.

Exemplar charts show the "thing" children are supposed to make or do: a completed math problem with an explanation, a sample of notes children might take during a science experiment, or a notebook entry of theories children have about a social studies inquiry question. In creating a vision of what the expectations are, teachers set what Charlotte Danielson calls "high expectations for products and effort" (Danielson, 2007). Just like a puzzle box helps you see where the pieces go, exemplar charts help students see how to put the pieces they have learned back into a coherent whole. As teachers, we work constantly to help our students become more independent thinkers. Exemplar charts support this work by providing clear goals that children can work toward independently. See Figure 5.1.

The difference between an exemplar chart and a work sample is in the annotations. Exemplar charts point out the skills, strategies, and habits that make the work successful and replicable. Kristi, a fan of fashion, loves looking at magazines and blogs that not only show people in

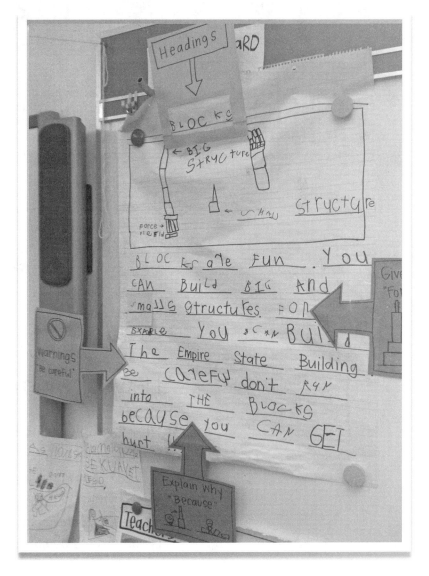

Figure 5.1 An annotated exemplar chart in information writing.

interesting outfits, but illuminate how and why they work (e.g., when wearing a voluminous skirt, keep your top structured and slim to avoid looking like a tent). Exemplars, therefore, give both a vision of what work is possible and expected as well as replicable tips to achieve the same work independently. Kristi does not need to buy *that* skirt and *that* top to create the same look, she just needs to remember: Voluminous skirt plus structured top equals fashion success. When exemplar charts have annotations, students are made aware that they do not need to copy that sentence; rather, they can keep the tip in mind that led to *that* sentence, and they can use that information to write their own sentence.

Exemplar charts can show one piece of work annotated, or show several pieces of work along a continuum of sophistication (i.e., a rubric as shown in Figure 5.2). High-quality rubrics present a sample of what work looks like along with annotations or indicators that explain why one sample is more or less sophisticated than the work around it. Visuals of the work enable children to hold their work up against the samples and say what their piece "looks" like, and the indicators help make explicit what they may need to add to make their work move along the progression. Exemplar charts communicate goals and expectations and illustrate the high level of work and effort students should attempt to achieve. When annotated, exemplars also provide clarity and support as children attempt to outgrow themselves and their work.

Figure 5.2 A rubric for reading independently.

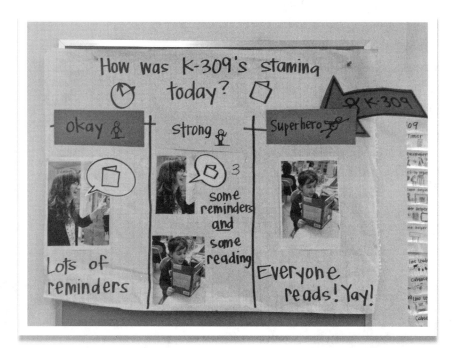

How Is It Made? How Is It Used?

How Exemplary Should an Exemplar Chart Be?

When working with teachers to create exemplars in writing, common questions include: "What work should I show?" "What annotations should I use?" "Should everything be spelled correctly?" All primary teachers (hopefully) know that a five-, six-, seven-, or eight-year-old is not going to be spelling every single word in the English language correctly. So should an example of the best writing possible in kindergarten show every word spelled correctly? This smart question underscores the tricky part of creating rubrics or exemplar charts. If we are creating a tool that aims to help children achieve the best work they possible can (with some scaffolding and teaching), what does a realistic exemplar look like?

For this thinking, we go back to two often relied upon resources: the work our children have created, and the CCSS. When creating a rubric to illustrate the continuum of math responses, for example, it makes sense for the first, most basic example on the rubric to look *slightly* stronger than what students are already doing, for the "on-grade-level" example to match what the standards ask, and for the highest-level example to reflect the standards for students in the grade above the one you teach.

An Annotated Attempt to Build a Math Exemplar Chart and Rubric

Making a rubric is not an easy process. It takes multiple people, attempts, and constant revision and reflection so that the rubric is informed by (and supports) the specific students you have, children in general at this developmental age, and the content you are teaching. Following is our annotated attempt at building a rubric around solving word problems for first grade.

The CCSS for Operations and Algebraic Thinking in Math state that first graders should:

> Solve word problems that call for addition of three whole numbers whose sum is less than or equal to 20, e.g., by using objects, drawings, and equations with a symbol for the unknown number to represent the problem.
>
> *(Common Core State Standards Initiative, Math 1.0A2. 2010)*

When looking over a standard, it can be helpful to underline key words and phrases—for example, note that the standard says *and*, not *or*, which indicates that children should be using all three methods to solve word problems, although not necessarily at the same time. Additionally, the standard goes out of its way to state that the child uses a symbol for the unknown number, which seems to be an attribute that might be overlooked when writing problems. Finally, this standard is for addition only with the key being three numbers and the maximum sum equaling twenty.

Looking closely at the standard has now given us enough information to make an exemplar chart (see Figure 5.3).

Many teachers make an exemplar chart and use that as a simple checklist or tool for children, saying, "Go check our classroom math example—do you have all the same parts?" However, some teachers may want to go further and indicate that there is a range of work on the way to creating work that is at the same level as that exemplar—and even a way to exceed it. Thus is born the rubric. A rubric must first be grounded in what your children are already doing—it's not helpful to show an example that is below the level of what students can do independently. Once you have a sense of the work your students in general can do, make the first level of the rubric contain the easiest or most accessible elements to lift the student work. In this case, depending on your actual students, it might be using a symbol and writing the signs.

Depending on how far your children are from the grade-level standard, you might find that you need another step that adds more of the elements into the rubric but does not yet meet standard. If your children are close, your next step on the rubric might be the grade-level standard. Remember, you likely have process charts that teach children how to do things like draw a picture, write an equation, and so on that they can refer to so they have a way to move from one step of the progression to the next.

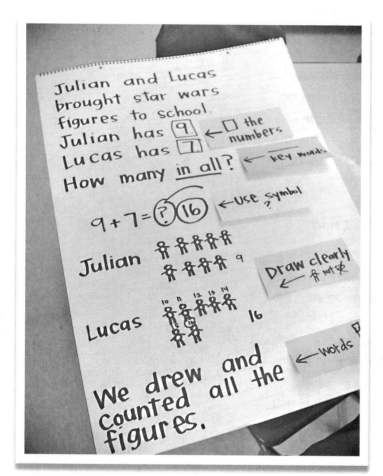

Figure 5.3 An annotated example for solving a word problem.

To continue building the rubric, we need more information. We could guess at what our students need to reach toward, but the CCSS lays it out for us. Look at the same category (Operations and Algebraic Thinking) for the next grade level. It says second graders should:

> Use addition and subtraction within 100 to solve one- and two-step word problems involving situations of adding to, taking from, putting together, taking apart, and comparing, with unknowns in all positions, e.g., by using drawings and equations with a symbol for the unknown number to represent the problem.
>
> *(Common Core State Standards Initiative, Second Grade 2010)*

Obviously, a lot happens in a year! To create a high-level exemplar that is right for your particular class, you may decide to pull some or all of these elements that are within their zone of proximal development when building the rubric. It is likely that your progression toward the standard, and beyond, will not look the same as other classes on the same grade. Classrooms are like snowflakes; no two are identical. When working with a tool that gives an endpoint, like the CCSS, the critical thinking work of the teacher is how the journey should progress for the students he or she teaches. Standards always need to be examined in relation to your very real students.

Writing Exemplars in the Content Areas

In *Smarter Charts,* we devote a whole section to the question of how to help students use the charts independently (Section 2, 28–59), and we begin by stressing the importance of "making charts with students, or with students in mind" (31). This goes for any kind of chart and for any subject you teach. Often, though, in content areas, bulletin boards have completed math pages, filled-in KWL (what you *know*, what you *want* to know, what you *learned*) charts, and other displays of worksheets that children have completed. This work has a place because it encourages children to organize their thinking and deepen their understandings of key concepts. Unfortunately, once this work is hung up, it is often forgotten, because it is not intended to support children's thinking; rather, it is intended to showcase their knowledge. We would like to suggest that it could become more effective and have a longer-lasting impact if some of this work was dissected by and with students for the thinking that was done so that it could be replicated again and again.

Thinking about this has led us to the process of selecting one piece of work, either a student's or the teacher's, and talking about it in depth. In math, this might be a completed word problem with an explanation that showcases quite a bit of effort and thinking; in writing, it might be a student's draft of a story. Frank Smith used the term "reading like a writer" in *Joining the Literacy Club* (1988). To turn a work example into an exemplar, we need to not only read it like a science writer, a math writer, a social studies writer, a sports writer, an art writer, a music writer, but we also need to name what we see and annotate the writing so that it becomes a learning tool rather than simply an example.

This also helps children more easily identify possible problems that might arise in any piece of writing. If as a class we have annotated a relevant section in a piece of science writing, such as "uses exact numbers," during a focused lesson on writing lab reports then, when a child looks at her own writing, she might notice that she does not use any numbers. She might then go back to her science notes to see if she wrote down any numbers in her observations or measurements that she can add to her writing, making it much clearer to the reader. Other possible annotations in science and social studies writing might describe and highlight the use of:

- descriptive details
- ordered steps
- specific examples
- clear pictures or diagrams
- specific vocabulary
- asking a question
- giving reasons.

Another thing to point out is that the piece of writing you are studying will be from an experiment or an inquiry the class has already completed, so students won't be inclined to directly copy the content. The piece itself may have been initially generated as class shared writing, a teacher's model, or a student example you have selected for this purpose. The process of rereading and annotating is intended to highlight the craft, thinking, and organization of the piece, but not the actual experiment, since the class has most likely moved forward to other experiments and inquiries. Often this work of noticing and anno-tating occurs as a focused lesson before children go off to work on something similar so they carry with them the essentials of the work they should be doing. This piece, this annotated piece, then becomes a true mentor text to use as a model for any kind of lab report the children may write in the future. The "Charts in Action" that follows takes us through such an experience.

CHARTS IN ACTION: USING AN EXEMPLAR WHEN WRITING A LAB REPORT IN SCIENCE

Lesson Focus: Read like a science writer and name ways a piece of writing is crafted to be effective and clear.

The focus of this whole-class lesson is to underscore the qualities of effective lab reports the teacher has taught during science and to help children use the repertoire chart to annotate the exemplar, thus reinforcing the strategies on the repertoire chart and creating a model children can use to reflect upon and create goals for their own science writing. Involving children in the actual annotations increases engagement and retention of what you are teaching and also provides valuable practice at looking beyond the content of writing to see the structure and elaboration underneath. Building grade-level expectations together also sets the stage for creating a rubric with one level above and one level below. Betsy Rupp Fulwiler in *Writing in Science in Action* (2011) suggests three key elements to consider when teaching children to write about their scientific inquiries: science concepts (constructing understanding), scientific thinking (fact-based, question-driven), and scientific skills (ability to observe, investigate, and use tools like scientists do). Depending on the needs of your class, you may choose to annotate any of these, along with basic structure and organizational tips. This lesson takes place during the time designated for science instruction to make the transfer of writing skills clear, but separate from the actual experiments or observations.

Materials

- **The repertoire chart for writing science lab reports**
- **An example of a lab report that has qualities listed on the chart**
- **Copies of lab report—one for each partnership or table group**
- **Paper and/or sticky notes and markers to add annotations**
- **Chart paper**

Marjorie begins the lesson by highlighting all the work the children have done to write like true scientists. Pointing to the repertoire chart, she says, ***"You have learned that scientists use several strategies to make sure writing is used to record detailed observations, to pursue questions and wonderings, and to develop theories about their investigations. Today I'm going to teach you how to use the strategies on our chart to help us look at a piece of science writing to see whether this example can become a model for our own writing."***

"Let's read the chart together to put the strategies back in our heads." The class does a choral reading of the chart—the heading and each bullet—as the teacher points to each line. **"Which strategies have you used in your own writing? Turn and tell your partner."**

Chart Tips

- Have the chart close to the example to be studied. See Figure 5.4.

- Put a copy of the exemplar piece on a document camera so everyone can see as you annotate it.

- Make sure the piece you have chosen has some obvious examples of the strategies listed on the repertoire chart.

- Use charts as an opportunity to engage in more shared reading (which also helps keep the charts current and known).

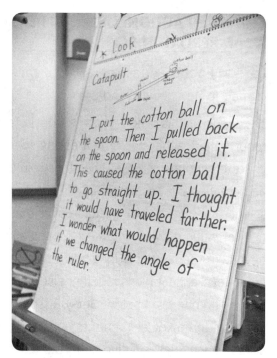

Figure 5.4 The piece of writing to be studied.

The children turn and share. **"Okay, now let's take a look at this lab report and look to see what this scientist has done to make her writing clear and strong. This is the part that describes the results of her experiment."** Marjorie reads it once straight through. **"Now I'm going to read it again part by part, so we can take a closer look and name what we see this science writer doing."** Marjorie reads the first two sentences then pauses and looks at the chart. **"Hmm. What has she done here that helps us understand the experiment and her observations?"** She turns and looks expectantly at the students. See Figure 5.5.

"She said pulled back on the cotton ball," Emmanuel says.

"Is that important information to include, Emmanuel?" Marjorie asks.

Figure 5.5 Marjorie points to the chart as students turn and talk.

Figure 5.6 Marjorie annotates the chart.

Emmanuel tilts his head thoughtfully. **"I think so, cause then we know what she did."**

"Yes, and that is something we have on our chart here," Marjorie says pointing to the chart. She then writes, "includes exact actions" on a Post-it and sticks it near the line. See Figure 5.6.

"What else do you notice this writer is doing that we could do to make our science writing effective and clear?"

Chart Tips

- When possible, use the same color to underline or highlight the text as the color used to write the annotation on or with.

- Cross-check what the child says with the chart to see that this is a strategy the class has learned and is expected to use. If not, consider adding it to the repertoire chart.

"Okay, let's look again. What else do you notice? Turn and tell your partner what this writer is doing that makes her science writing so clear." The children all turn and talk while the teacher listens in.

"Minds back. So what else are you seeing?"

"She drew the picture and labeled it," Andrea offers.

"And she asks questions about what would happen if they moved the ruler," Michael adds.

"Do you think those are all important things to include when writing about an observation?" Marjorie asks the class. They all nod and shout out **"Yes!"**

"Why?" Marjorie responds.

"We will know more," Jose says.

"Yes, writing that includes important details helps us all to know more. And that's why this is important work you are doing. You are really looking closely and thinking about what science writers can do to share their observations and to grow their thinking. I'm going to give each of you a copy of this science

CHARTS IN ACTION

report, and I want you and your partner to label all the things you think are important to include in a science report, using the chart to help you. Then we will get back together to share. Ready? Okay, off you go!"

Chart Tips

- Make small copies of the charts you want students to look more closely at and use more often.

- Set children up to do inquiry work using charts as a guide.

- Give children sticky notes, paper, or highlighters and let children mark up the exemplar.

- Using sticky notes allows for movement from one piece to another and shows how craft moves can be used in many places.

At the end of the session, Marjorie calls the children back together to share each group's noticings and annotations. As each group shares, Marjorie annotates the science writing, which she has posted on a piece of chart paper. This allows plenty of room for the labels and captions to be displayed. See Figure 5.7.

Next Steps

Each student can return to her own science notebook and self-assess the quality of the writing based on the discussion that has evolved from studying an exemplar. A session such as this can lead children to reflect and to develop goals that are based on what has been taught (and therefore attainable to each and all).

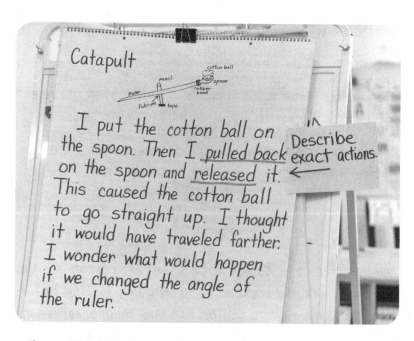

Figure 5.7 A close-up on the first annotation.

Exemplar Charts Across the Content Areas

We keep referring to that ancient quote, "A picture is worth a thousand words," because it holds true in so many ways. A picture is universal because it is not dependent upon knowing any one language or graphic form. Pictures can be an inspiration: They give us images that might be different from the images we have created in our own minds, or reinforce and strengthen our own mental images. An exemplar chart provides such a picture for our students. Whether it is a sample piece of writing, a map, a tool, or a photograph, the exemplar gives children an image of what something can look like while highlighting the key ingredients that make it effective. Children then consider the similarities and differences between the exemplar and their own work and are inspired to try things they might not have thought to do, or perhaps have forgotten to do. And that is a beautiful thing to see happening in the classroom, in any content area.

Social Studies Focus: Observing a Photograph and Naming Expectations in a Community of Respect

Rationale

In the beginning of the year in primary grades, the most common social studies unit is building and understanding the classroom community. This is often done through discussions of expectations and habits that will be mutually beneficial to students and teachers. However, discussions are not the only way to establish the ground rules of a community. Studying a photograph closely is a form of inquiry that encourages thinking and curiosity, but the ability to name what is seen clearly and specifically is a skill that requires modeling and practice. Putting a photograph up so the whole class can see it, talk about it, then label it not only allows for this practice, but you create an example of what this kind of inquiry can look and sound like, as well as establishing an exemplar of "listening with respect." See Figure 5.8.

Figure 5.8 A chart from Katie Lee's classroom that shows an example of listening respectfully.

Decisions That Can Be in the Hands of Children

While the teacher guides the inquiry, children are asked to make many decisions about what to notice and what words to use. The teacher guides their choices by asking questions, such as, "What do you notice

---

Social Studies Exemplar Chart Possibilities

★ "Ways We Can Use a Map to Learn About Our World"

★ "How We Are Great Citizens in the Cafeteria"

★ "Thank-You Letters Matter"

★ "Field Trip Notes"

---

in this picture that supports our community of respect? How do you know this child is listening?" Though the teacher may have some ideas in mind, it is ultimately the children that name the parts that should be replicated by the class as a whole (hence, Katie's class ended up with a Magic Six and not the Magic Five more commonly seen in primary classrooms that prompt children to sit with legs crossed, hands in lap, eyes on teacher, mouth closed, and ears listening).

Next Steps

This kind of exemplar can help a child self-regulate his own behavior. Now that there is a visual model of what listening looks like, a child can take himself through a mental checklist of his own body. Additionally, once the children have done this type of close observation with you a few times, they will be ready to do it more independently, perhaps first with a small group or a partnership. They can then use the photographs they annotate to have discussions where they explain not only what they see, but what this makes them think and wonder. They can develop theories and questions that might lead them to further inquiries and investigations.

Science Focus: Revising a Theory When You Get More Information

Rationale

One of the beautiful aspects of young children is their confidence. Children often know something is true just because they think something is true. Revision of ideas is a challenging and critical part of the primary grades. One way to support children in making revisions is to highlight, through exemplar thinking, when a child changes her idea as she gets more information. When something is highlighted in this way, it suddenly becomes the en vogue activity in the classroom. When an old idea is abandoned or changed to embrace growth in thinking, we are teaching children to be flexible and curious about their preconceived notions. Highlighting that the old idea (the machine is an excavator) and replacing it with a new idea (it's actually a digger, which is a specific type of excavator) after further study makes an example of the kind of reflective thinking we want children to do.

Figure 5.9 A kindergarten chart about revising theories.

Decisions That Can Be in the Hands of Children

Children can define what revision means based on their understanding of the process. In this classroom, children identified revision as something changing, but in other classrooms the language selected by children might sound different. Starting with children's natural language (*something changed*) gives a place to attach the more academic terms (*revision*). See Figure 5.9.

Next Steps

Revision without justification simply seems like a substitution, rather than a thoughtful evolution of an idea. The next step is for children to explain how they came to the decision that their old idea was no longer working, and the new one is more accurate. When working with children whose thinking outpaces their motor skills, this justification may take place in the form of conversation, illustration, or labeling.

Science Exemplar Chart Possibilities

★ "How to Write Up an Experiment"

★ "Setting Up for an Experiment"

★ "Making a Scientific Table Clear and Organized"

Math Focus: Writing an Explanation for Solving a Word Problem

Rationale

When asked to "show your work," children need to have a vision for what that might look like in mathematics. Being able to explain clearly how a solution was attained is an important skill that requires much modeling. Looking at students' written explanations for how a story problem was solved will enable them to see some ways to make thinking clear and also encourage them to think critically to make suggestions about how to revise the piece to make it even better. See Figure 5.10.

Decisions That Can Be in the Hands of Children

First asking "What are some ways this mathematician explained her thinking?" sets the children up to read a mathematical explanation

---

Math Exemplar Chart Possibilities

★ "Writing a Math Journal Entry"

★ "Look How We Set Up for a Math Game!"

★ "Using Mathematical Vocabulary"

Figure 5.10 An example of persistence in math.

Other Curricular Areas

A picture is not only worth a thousand words, but it provides a vision of what is expected and possible, no matter the subject being learned.

★ Art: "Ways a Painting Uses Line, Shape, and Color"
★ Music: "Check Your Finger Placement on the Recorder"
★ Gym: "Perfect Position for a Safe Jump"

closely and critically. The teacher's role is only to guide the conversation as needed and to act as the scribe recording their observations.

Next Steps

Partners can do this same kind of close reading with each other's written explanations using the exemplar chart as a guide. This will set them up to have mathematical discussions that go beyond simply saying an answer is right or wrong. They will also become more aware of how important it is to be clear in your explanations.

Last Words

In the Italian preprimary schools in the Reggio Emilia district of Italy, the environment is considered the third educator, alongside the teachers and the parents. The educators in Reggio Emilia have successfully shown that everything surrounding children becomes an influential model—teachers, parents, fellow students, the classroom environment. The exemplar charts that are hanging in each of our classrooms are an integral part of this environment and can have a powerful effect on children when we teach students to use them. Not only do they record the effects of our teaching, but they become powerful models for children to look toward and mentor themselves toward.

Models and mentors are valuable assets when it comes to learning how to do something even better. We often think about "mentor authors" when teaching revision and craft in writing as students work toward publishing—sharing their work with a targeted audience. But mentors and models are useful no matter what it is you are trying to

make better, whether improving your writing or your home decorating skills. Donald Crews and HGTV have one thing in common—they both provide models that not only inspire but also make the task at hand seem accessible and doable.

Models and mentors provide a vision and a pathway for how something can go no matter the subject. Students can look at their own writing alongside the exemplars and use the exemplars to give partners compliments and tips for how to make their thinking and explanations more efficient and effective. This will lead to increased confidence because they have been allowed to take risks and try ideas out.

Exemplars and rubrics are the tools that help children see what they are learning in context. Just as we can use strategies to help us put puzzles together (look for the corner pieces, put the edges down first, put pieces where they might go as you find them), we can teach strategies to help students achieve *any* new thing. However, it is having the final image in mind, the exemplar, the puzzle box cover, that allows children to see the big picture and make sense of *why* these strategies matter. See Figure 5.11.

Figure 5.11 Thinking in action.

Figure 5.12 Have fun, and happy charting!

Last, Last Words

Over the years of working with teachers and students around charts and visible learning, we have realized that what we talk about when we discuss charting is bigger than anything you could put on a chart with pen. Charts help clarify our own thinking and in turn make our teaching clearer to our students by showing them multiple entry points and ways for doing things. In this book, we developed names and descriptions for different kinds of charts to make it easier to talk about the various pathways of learning and thinking that we present to our students. A chart is never *just* a chart, as you have seen throughout this book.

Sometimes we want charts to teach children ways to make their life more organized and efficient. We call these "routine charts," but really they are a model for living life in a way that minimizes wasted time and maximizes thinking and learning time. They help make repetitive actions become automatic and invisible, which allows the brain to explore and discover the more complex. See Figure 5.12.

When we teach vocabulary and big ideas, we call these "concept charts," but they are so much more. These charts illustrate for children that "facts" are never static, that learners constantly revise their thinking, and that recording what you learn is a surefire way to reflect and grow even more thinking. Concept charts underscore that what really matters is not what you know, but how you use what you know to learn more.

"Process charts" may break down a specific skill into manageable steps, but really these charts say: This thing you thought was hard is not; you just have to try it one step at a time. These charts may help children study photos or solve a word problem, but they also illustrate that you can tackle just about anything if you start at the first step. Understanding that all you do is a process opens possibilities to children that might have been thought impossible before.

"Repertoire charts" are about possibility, flexibility, and resilience. The charts may model the different ways a scientist can gather more information, but more importantly they say that there are lots of ways to do things and you have the power to make the decisions about which way will work best for you. Teaching children to be flexible, consider options, and most importantly, try, try, again is work that will carry them far in life.

Last, but not least, "exemplar charts" serve as a model for children of the work and thinking they should aspire to in the classroom. The message implicit in this is that we all have models we look to in life and that one way to learn, to grow, and to thrive is to look to models of success with admiration and ask, "What of this could I try?" "What can I do to grow as a scientist, mathematician, social scientist, artist, musician, or person?" Sometimes a vision of what is possible is all we need.

Charts, at first glance, are deceptively cute, often simple-looking pieces of paper. But as with many things in the world of education, charts' appearance belies a critical message. Distilling the complex into the simple is no easy task. We make charts, not for wallpaper, but for the message: There is no limit to what you can achieve and become, and these are tools that will support you on your journey.

How to help children become independent thinkers and problem solvers across the day is not a mission accomplished in a single book; rather, it is a conversation that will continue. We look forward to having it with you through our twitter (@chartchums) and our blog (chartchums.wordpress.com) and by hearing how you have made this work even smarter, too.

Until then, have fun and happy charting!

Kristi Mraz

Marjorie Martinelli

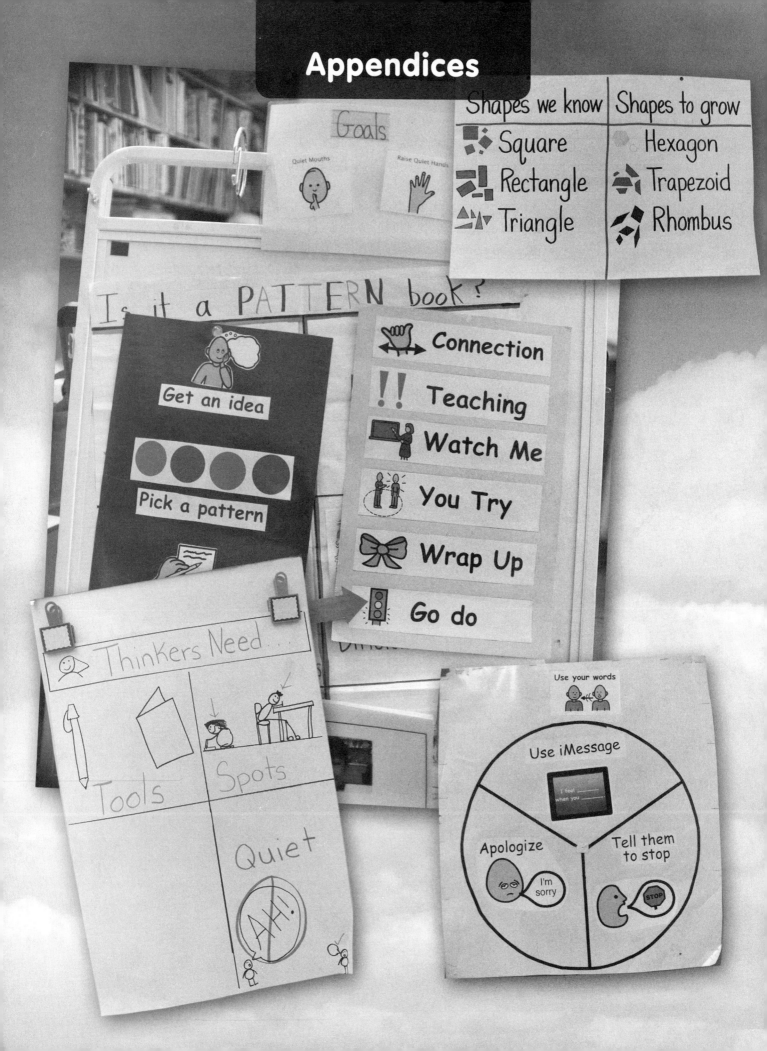

Unit Planning with Charts in Mind

Unit name:	
Start date:	End date/celebration:

Big ideas and questions of the unit:

Standards met:

Teaching to support big ideas/question 1:	Chart:
Teaching to support big ideas/question 2:	Chart:
Teaching to support big ideas/question 3:	Chart:

Appendix A

Figure A.1 Keeping charts in mind can help you plan.

A Field Guide to Content Charts

Type of Chart	Purpose	Notes	Example
1. Routine	Teaches a routine or behavior to students	• Often numbered • Written like a how-to • Includes photographs of students in action • Most often made at the beginning of the year	Figure 1.1 (p. 1)
2. Genre and Concept	Records key concepts or vocabulary of the genre or the content being studied	• Usually built collaboratively with students after studying a genre or concept • Grows over multiple lessons • Often includes content-specific vocabulary	Figure 2.1 (p. 19)
3. Process	Breaks a big skill into a sequence of steps	• Can be numbered or represented in a circle • Students need to do each of the steps to complete the process • Usually taught in one lesson	Figure 3.1 (p. 41)
4. Repertoire	Lists several strategies for a big skill	• Not numbered • Students self-select the strategy that matches what they need to do • Grows over multiple lessons • Smaller versions are often given out to students or put on tables	Figure 4.1 (p. 58)
5. Exemplar	Shows an annotated example that can be used as a mentor	• The example comes from a student, the teacher, or a published text, illustration, or photograph • Teacher and students annotate together as they discuss key elements	Figure 5.1 (p. 71)

Figure B.1 Knowing the type of charts helps plan for effective instruction.

Helpful Resources

Books

There are a world of books that we could suggest reading in addition to what's listed in the bibliography. Below are a few that we found particularly helpful to our thinking about teaching in the content areas.

A Quick Guide to Boosting Language Acquisition in Choice Time, by Alison Porcelli and Cheryl Tyler, Heinemann (2008)

Tools of the Mind, by Elena Bodrova and Deborah Leong, Pearson (2006)

Young Mathematicians at Work Series by Cathy Twomey Fosnot, Heinemann (2001–2010)

A Collection of Math Lessons, by Marilyn Burns and Bonnie Tank, Scholastic (1991)

Looking Closely and Listening Carefully: Learning Literacy Through Inquiry, by Heidi Mills, Timothy O'Keefe, and Louise B. Jennings, NCTE (2004)

Young Investigators: The Project Approach in the Early Years, by Judy Harris Help and Lillian Katz, Teachers College Press (2010)

Black Ants and Buddhists, by Mary Cowhey, Stenhouse (2006)

Apps

There is no end to the ways technology can improve charting; below are just a few of the apps we have found helpful in our own work.

iFontMaker: Make your own font and use it on any computer.

Pic Stitch: Create a collage of pictures to use on a chart.

Snap: Annotate photos and print them out.

audio Boo: Capture audio and store it online for others to hear.

Qrafter Pro: Generate your own QR codes to use on your charts or with student work

Twitter: Connect with other educators (and us: @chartchums, @Marjorie_ Writes, @MrazKristine.

Websites and Blogs

There is an infinite number of resources on the Web; here are a few that we visit frequently.

These are bloggers that talk about a diverse set of topics, but are connected by one thing—a passion for student centered teaching:

- www.christopherlehman.wordpress.com
- www.kateandmaggie.com
- www.choiceliteracy.com
- www.mattbgomez.com
- www.kinderconfidential.wordpress.com
  (including our own) www.chartchums.wordpress.com

These website have resources to support teachers:

- www.nzmaths.co.nz
- www.k-5mathteachingresources.com
- www.discoveryeducation.com/teachers
- www.heinemann.com/digitalcampus

Bibliography

Afflerbach, Peter, P. David Pearson, and Scott G. Pearson. 2008. "Clarifying Differences Between Reading Skills and Reading Strategies." *The Reading Teacher* 61 (5): 364–73.

Banilower, E. R., Smith, P. S., Weiss, I. R., Malzahn, K. A., Campbell, K. M., and Weis, A. M. 2013. Report of the 2012 National Survey of Science and Mathematics Education. Chapel Hill, NC: Horizon Research, Inc.

Beck, Isabel, et al. 2002. *Bringing Words to Life: Robust Vocabulary Instruction.* New York: Guilford Press.

Bruner, Jerome. 1966. *Toward a Theory of Instruction.* Cambridge, MA: The Belknap Press of Harvard University Press.

———. 1971. *The Relevance of Education.* New York: W. W. Norton & Company.

Calkins, Lucy. 2012. *Units of Study in Writing K–5*. Portsmouth, NH: Heinemann.

Cervetti, Jaynes, and Elfrieda Heibert. 2009. *Seeds of Science/Roots of Reading Project.* Berkeley, CA: University of California. Available at: www .scienceandliteracy.org.

Common Core State Standards Initiative (CCSS). 2010. www.corestandards.org /ELA-Literacy

Danielson, Charlotte. 2007. *Enhancing Professional Practice,* Second Edition. Alexandria, VA: Association for Supervision and Curriculum Development.

Dweck, Carol S. 2006. *Mindset: The New Psychology of Success.* New York: Ballantine Books.

Fulwiler, Betsy Rupp. 2011. *Writing in Science in Action.* Portsmouth, NH: Heinemann.

Gandini, Lella. 1998. "Educational and Caring Spaces." In *The Hundred Languages of Children: The Reggio Emilia Approach—Advanced Reflections*, edited by Carolyn Edwards, Lella Gandini, and George Forman. Westport, CT/London: Ablex.

Gladwell, Malcolm. 2011. *Outliers: The Story of Success.* New York: Back Bay Books.

Harvey, Stephanie, and Anne Goudvis. 2007. *Strategies That Work,* Second Edition. Portland, ME: Stenhouse Publishers.

Johnston, Peter. 2004. *Choice Words: How Our Language Affects Children's Learning.* Portland, ME: Stenhouse.

Kohn, Alfie. 1998. *What to Look for in a Classroom.* San Francisco, CA: Jossey-Bass.

Malaguzzi, Loris. 1998. "History, Ideas, and Basic Philosophy: An Interview with Lella Gandini." In *The Hundred Languages of Children: The Reggio Emilia Approach—Advanced Reflections*, edited by Carolyn Edwards, Lella Gandini, and George Forman. Westport, CT/London: Ablex.

Martinelli, Marjorie, and Kristine Mraz. 2012. *Smarter Charts: Optimizing an Instructional Staple to Create Independent Readers and Writers.* Portsmouth, NH: Heinemann.

McGinnis, Ellen. 2011. *Skill Streaming the Elementary School Child: A Guide for Teaching Prosocial Skills.* Champaign, IL: Research Press.

McTighe, Jay, and Grant Wiggins. 2005. *Understanding by Design.* Boston: Pearson Education.

The New York City Department of Education Social Studies Scope and Sequence K–8. 2008–2009. Available at: http://schools.nycenet.edu /offices/teachlearn/ss/SocStudScopeSeq.pdf

Pink, Daniel H. 2009. *Drive: The Surprising Truth About What Motivates Us.* New York: Penguin.

Smith, Frank. 1988. *Joining the Literacy Club.* Portsmouth, NH: Heinemann.

Tough, Paul. 2012. *How Children Succeed: Grit, Curiosity, and the Hidden Power of Character.* Boston: Houghton Mifflin Harcourt.

Notes/Sketches

Notes/Sketches

Notes/Sketches

Notes/Sketches

Notes/Sketches

Notes/Sketches

Notes/Sketches